THE EURO-BANK

THE EURO-BANK: ITS ORIGINS, MANAGEMENT AND OUTLOOK

Steven I. Davis

A HALSTED PRESS BOOK

JOHN WILEY & SONS
New York

First published in the United Kingdom 1976 by
THE MACMILLAN PRESS LTD
London and Basingstoke

Published in the U.S.A.
by Halsted Press, a Division
of John Wiley & Sons, Inc.
New York.

Printed in Great Britain

Library of Congress Cataloging in Publication Data

Davis, Steven I
    The Euro-bank, its origins, management, and out-
look.

    "A Halsted Press book."
    1. Banks and banking, International.   2. Euro-
dollar market.   I. Title.
G3897.D38   332.1'5   76-15912
ISBN 0-470-15060-2

To my mother and father for setting the example

Contents

Preface

Writing one's first book is an awesome task. Despite the presumed advantage in this particular case of a professional familiarity with the international banking community, this particular author has run the emotional gamut over the past year from panic at stating the obvious to exhilaration at rediscovering the wheel. On balance, I will be more than satisfied if this book provides some useful insight for those in industry, government, academic pursuits — and even banking! — interested in the management behaviour and strategic issues of today's generation of new international banks. My thanks go first to Macmillan for giving me the opportunity to express these views and specifically to T. M. Farmiloe for his personal assistance to a novice author.

The active and generous assistance of a number of banking colleagues, professors and friends has made this book possible. Geoffrey Bell of Schroders provided the original inspiration and a helping hand throughout. Professor L. S. Pressnell almost single-handedly furnished the bibliography for Chapter 1 and helped provide an invaluable historical perspective. Professor Charles Williams of the Harvard Business School focused my attention on the key issues — as he has done for me since my student days. Michael von Clemm of Credit Suisse White Weld, Stani Yassukovitch of European Banking Company and Fred Klopstock of the Federal Reserve staff — all authors as well as bankers — provided helpful advice and took the time from their busy careers to read my final manuscript. Friends at the Bank of England, the World Bank, Federal Reserve staff and other organisations helped locate useful statistical data. The editorial staff of the *Banker* not only shared their data library with me but also were kind enough to produce some specific tables for use in the book, and David Ashby of Bankers Trust contributed his usual thoughtful analysis of the structure of the Euromarkets.

I am particularly indebted to forty senior London Euro-bank executives whose comments in extensive confidential interviews provided the basis for the bulk of Chapters 3, 4 and 5. They gave willingly of their time and spoke frankly about their management policies, and I can only hope I faithfully transcribed their thoughts.

Finally, I want to thank my colleagues at First International Bancshares: my directors in Dallas, Texas for their vision and understanding support; my colleagues in London for their helpful comments in editing the book and developing statistical information, and particularly my secretary, Amy McMullin, for her usual patience and good humour in expertly translating my scrawl to a final typescript.

London   STEVEN I. DAVIS
October 1975

Introduction and Overview

The purpose of this book, quite simply, is to analyse today's generation of Euro-banks from the perspective of management to determine how these banks are dealing with the critical issues they face in the mid-1970s. The Eurobond and Eurocurrency markets centred in London have been the objects of extensive research and analysis by scholars, journalists and practitioners focusing on such sectors as economic theory and practice, market evolution and structure, and lending and investing practices. For an excellent coverage of these and other aspects of the Euromarkets, the reader is referred to recent volumes by Paul Einzig, Geoffrey Bell, Brian Scott Quinn and the Robert Morris Associates/Bankers Association for Foreign Trade.[1]

Relatively little attention, however, has been devoted in the current literature to the separately capitalised, specialised banking institutions which have grown up with the market since the early 1960s. This book will attempt to describe some of the historical precedents for these institutions, the rationale for their establishment, their activities and objectives, and, in some detail, the conduct of asset and liability management as well as activities which do not relate directly to the balance sheet. There is nothing in this book that will significantly raise the learning curves of bankers active in the Euromarkets, but the consolidation in one volume of a body of management practices and the issues faced by Euro-bank management will hopefully have some value to those interested in management behaviour as well as the factors which will determine the future of these banks.

Euro-banks, rather than branches or other overseas operations of existing national banks, have been selected for analysis as their experience brings into focus more sharply many of today's issues in international banking because of the heavy concentration of their activity in the Euromarkets. While relatively unimportant in terms of market share, these banks in many respects are 'pure' international banks because of this Euromarket concentration. In addition, they are relatively free from the domestic influences which may dominate the behaviour of an overseas branch of an international bank. While this choice creates definitional problems which cannot be entirely resolved, the use of a sufficiently broad sample of Euro-banks should minimise these problems.

My focus throughout is on how management deals with the major issues confronting banks operating primarily in the Eurocurrency market, and an attempt is made to define these issues. The book concludes with an effort to describe the factors which will influence Euro-banks in the future and to enumerate a few likely trends for Euro-banks individually as a market sector. As a by-product of the Euromarket boom of the 1960s and early 1970s, the Euro-bank in some cases was a fashionable, contemporary aspect of a national bank's overseas expansion programme; once established, however, most of these banks have developed a momentum and character of their own.

In addition to my own direct experience in the market since 1970, I have used as source material the bulk of the literature in English on the specific activities of international banks since the Middle Ages; recent books on Euromarket structure, theory and practice; and current statistical data published by international bodies such as the Bank for International Settlements and World Bank Group as well as such national authorities as the Federal Reserve Board and Bank of England. To supplement this data, I have also undertaken to compile 1973 and 1974 statistics on the financial performance of a sample of forty London-based Euro-banks to reflect actual management practice in terms of such key variables and measures of performance as gearing, asset composition, liquidity and return on assets and capital. While the selection of the sample necessarily involved making arbitrary distinctions, an attempt was made to select as large a group as possible of banks which had been established or restructured since the mid-1960s largely to participate directly or indirectly in the London Euromarkets. In practice, the sample includes primarily consortium banks, or institutions owned by two or more other financial institutions, and banks wholly-owned by a single such institution. They are all authorised by the Bank of England to deal in foreign currencies and derive most of their income from operations in the London market; the great majority are also incorporated in the UK. As UK banks they may carry on a sterling deposit and lending activity, but in most cases this is quite limited.

Finally, to supplement my own personal management experience and views, I conducted reasonably extensive interviews on management policies, issues and objectives with the senior management — generally the chief executive — of forty Euro-banks whose activities are conducted primarily in the London market. With one exception, all the banks in the statistical sample are included in the interview sample. The results of these interviews must be qualified by the usual caveats applied to any 'on the record' comments dealing often with confidential information, but the assurance of anonymity to the interviewees and the emphasis on policies rather than confidential specifics discussed with a fellow member of the banking profession hopefully produced some useful results.

Perhaps the most arbitrary of the lines which had to be drawn to produce a reasonably concise, well-documented and issue-oriented volume on management practices was my decision to centre the analytical portion of the book on Euro-banks whose major operational centre is London. The large number of international banks set up with similar objectives and operating primarily in financial centres such as Luxembourg, Singapore, Hong Kong, Paris, Brussels and Geneva have thereby been excluded from my statistical analysis and the management interviews. While this volume could perhaps better be entitled 'The London Euro-bank', such a focus on London can be justified on several grounds. London is not only the acknowledged international financial centre in terms of size, depth and virtually any other criterion, but it also is the operating base for a larger number of Euro-banks than any other centre. London-based banks tend to be older, larger and have a more useful statistical track record than those in these newer centres. While Euro-banks in other centres often have a different strategy, set of priorities or regulatory climate than a London Euro-bank, the basic management issues and banking practices are usually quite similar, in large part because the London marketplace plays such a dominant role in the world-wide Euromarkets in such key activities as funding, pricing and loan syndication. Finally, statistical information available for the London market as a whole as well as for individual Euro-banks is more informative than for other Euromarket centres. Nevertheless, a future volume could well explore the particular circumstances and management issues of banks in centres such as Singapore or Luxembourg.

More specifically, Chapter 1 provides a historical perspective for today's Euro-bank. While this is not an attempt to provide an authoritative, thorough history of international banking, an effort is made for three specific periods of international banking history to describe the structure, practice and objectives of new banks set up primarily to engage in international banking. A particular effort is made to focus on management practices of earlier institutions in terms of lending policies, types of borrowers, lending instruments, financial ratios, security obtained, loss experience, source of deposits and ultimate financial performance. Given the limited literature available on such micro-economic subjects, this analysis is necessarily spotty, but at a minimum the reader should be aware that today's generation of Euro-banks is not without historical precedents and that the experience of these antecedents may shed some light on the current operations and future of the Euro-banks.

Chapter 2 describes the development of the Euro-bank itself as an institution. Following a very brief summary of the evolution and structure of the Eurocurrency markets, this chapter analyses the location, statistical importance, ownership, objectives, activities, and management background of the Eurobanking community.

The analysis of specific management policies is begun in Chapter 3, which centres on asset management. The principal asset components are described, and the relationship of the major categories of interbank loans and customer loans is analysed. Particular attention is paid to the management of the loan portfolio to maximise return and minimise losses.

Such factors as risk diversification, credit standards, maturity controls, interest margin objectives, loan loss reserves, sources of business and decision making processes are analysed in some detail.

Chapter 4 focuses on liability, or money, management and capital adequacy. The importance and nature of deposits from other banks is studied in detail, and available data on the time mismatch between assets and liabilities are analysed. The decision making process as it relates to the granting of interbank lines is discussed in the context of the vulnerability of a Euro-bank's deposits to loss of confidence in the market. The results of the 1974 crisis of confidence are studied in terms of parent support, differentiation of rates paid by banks, the different approaches taken to build a deposit base outside the interbank market, and the perceived need to participate in the market both as a lender and borrower of funds. The strategic role of a Euro-bank's dealing room is analysed along with the attitude toward dealing profitability and risk and the management controls placed on foreign exchange and deposit mismatch positions. Attitudes toward capital adequacy are discussed.

Non-deposit and lending operations are covered in Chapter 5, which discusses among others the investment or merchant banking activities Euro-banks have undertaken to improve their return on invested funds or carry out objectives established by parent banks. These include the management of syndicated loans, participation in the various aspects of the Eurobond market or private placements of fixed interest obligations, corporate financial services, the taking of equity interests and other activities. Special attention is focused on the motivation of Euro-banks in deciding whether or not to undertake these non-commercial banking activities, the factors which appear to be vital for success, and the results obtained to date.

Chapter 6 examines the financial performance in recent years of a statistical sample of forty banks in the London market. On the basis of the published statements of these banks, the key ratios of gearing, liquidity, loans to deposits and capital funds and return on capital and assets are analysed. An attempt is made to relate performance to such factors as age of bank, the profitability goals stated by management in interviews and the profitability of non-Euro-banks.

The issues arising from Euro-bank experience to date are defined and discussed in Chapter 7. The boom period through mid-1974 is contrasted with the sharp reversal of market conditions following the shocks to confidence experienced in the summer of 1974 with an emphasis on Euro-banks in particular. The problems of evaluation of international project and sovereign risk credits are reviewed together with the limited amount of information available with regard to actual loss experience to date. The issue of adequate funding is discussed in the context of the measures being taken to resolve the problem. The issue of providing an adequate return on invested funds is reviewed in the framework of the objectives of stockholders, and the contingent liability or responsibility on the part of the parent for the Euro-bank affiliate is discussed as a forth issue. A final issue is the ability of Euro-banks to develop a significant investment banking or fee-based income.

The concluding chapter discusses the outlook for Euro-banks. A distinction is made between, on the one hand, the two exogenous factors of the development of the Euromarkets themselves and the status and priorities of individual parent institutions, and on the other, those factors which can be significantly influenced by management itself. Continued growth of the Euromarkets is projected although a slowdown in international trade and investment and periodic crises of confidence will influence Euro-bank development to a significant extent. Stockholder attitudes in the context of actual performance and the ownership structure of the Euro-banks will result in the restructuring of many Euro-banks, and the ability of stockholders to make a business contribution will be a major factor in determining future performance. Key factors by which management performance should be judged are discussed. Finally, a number of likely trends in range of services, profitability and physical location are reviewed.

1 Some Earlier Patterns in International Banking

The Eurodollar market and the institutions it has spawned represent a unique phase of international banking development. There are, however, a number of periods since the Middle Ages when factors such as the growth of international trade and investment produced a variety of new banking institutions whose objectives, lending practices, market environment, sponsorship and structure were not at all dissimilar to the Euro-banks established in the 1960s and 1970s.

The behaviour of these institutions and their relative success in achieving objectives offer at a minimum a useful historical perspective with which to begin this book. The chapter which follows does not purport to be a thoroughgoing and fully researched history of international banking nor an intensive, systematic micro-analysis of banking behaviour through the ages. It does, however, summarise very roughly three periods of international banking history during which a novel combination of new banking institutions, financing techniques, or financial markets arose in response to a surge in cross-border lending and investment.

As the available literature on banking behaviour and policies which is our principal interest is quite limited, the following chapter has severe limitations from an analytical standpoint. It provides, however, a useful historical perspective for today's Euro-bank, particularly for the practitioner who is understandably fully involved in the challenges and opportunities of managing a Euro-bank in the mid-1970s. For such a reader, no attempt has been made to draw parallels with contemporary experience, although Chapter 8 does relate some of the historical themes of international banking to today's problems. For the reader familiar with banking history and interested solely in current issues, however, an invitation is extended to commence one's reading with Chapter 2 of this book.

Renaissance Merchant Bankers: the Medici and Fugger

The fifteenth and sixteenth centuries in Europe witnessed the growth — and demise — of merchant banking dynasties who financed international trade, created foreign exchange markets, met the voracious financial needs of national rulers and the Papacy, and established new industrial and trade ventures. Starting from a slender capital base supplemented to a limited extent by deposits from the clergy and wealthy noblemen, these family-owned and managed banks grew through retained earnings to establish foreign subsidiaries and representative offices throughout Europe.

Given the proliferation of currencies — metal and paper, good and bad — and the religious prohibition against usury, the trade financing function in the fifteenth century almost inevitably involved a foreign exchange risk. Typically a Florentine bank lending to an Italian importing from England would buy from him for local currency a draft drawn in sterling on a London correspondent; the sterling proceeds would be used to purchase a bill on Florence to repay the lending bank. The selling rate of the initial bill would be fixed so that, at the then current exchange rate, the proceeds of the second bill would produce the desired interest return to the lender. If exchange rates changed in the three to four months needed to complete the transaction, either the banker or his borrower lost out. In addition to providing the necessary foreign exchange, such a transaction was not considered usury by the church as the lender was carrying a certain foreign exchange risk. In addition, the bank stood to lose money if the drawer of the initial bill would not pay, the correspondent bank failed to make the funds available, or if the remittance bill purchased was uncollectable.

The other traditional form of lending during this period was a short or medium-term direct extension of credit to an individual ruler, Pope, or member of the nobility or clergy. These were generally made on a fixed rate, fully secured basis with collateral consisting of jewels and other saleable personal assets, customs or tax receipts or the proceeds of sales of products such as copper or silver from royal or Papal monopolies.

In addition to their lending activities, the Renaissance merchant bankers sold goods on consignment and invested for their own account in the manufacture and shipment of commodities such as alum, wool, silk and spices. The Medici owned wool and silk factories which made a small contribution to overall profits, while about 20 per cent of the Fugger bank's assets in 1546 represented stock in trade of copper and cloth.[1] The Medici controlled partnerships which operated on a royalty basis the Papal alum mines at Tolfa and the iron mines on Elba, both of which represented regional monopolies.

Established in 1397 in Florence, the Medici Bank was the most important of its time, whereas Florence was the leading banking centre in the fourteenth and fifeenth centuries. Its larger predecessors in the fourteenth century — the Bardi and Peruzzi — had been liquidated following defaults on extensive loans to monarchs such as Edward III of England Robert of Naples. Branches were established in the first half of the fifteenth century in Rome, Venice, Milan, Pisa, Avignon, Bruges, London and Geneva. Each branch was generally separately capitalised with funds provided by the local manager on a minority basis and the Medici family-controlled partnerships in Florence as majority stockholders. The local manager was compensated on a performance basis with a share of profits greater than his proportion of paid-in equity. This unique network functioned as an integrated unit by providing borrowing facilities to other branches, collecting remittances and drawing on other branches for trade financing requirements. Rome branch, which provided liquidity for the system by tapping Papal deposits, also provided over half the consolidated bank's profits during the early part of the fifteenth century.[2] Some deposits were also provided by wealthy individuals, who received interest on an 'as and when earned' basis to avoid charges of usury.

While no consolidated figures are available, it appears that non-stock-holder deposits represented a multiple of up to ten times capital for individual branches. Fixed rate deposits could be acquired from money markets such as Antwerp on the basis of the Medici's prime name. Such deposits generally cost from 8—10 per cent per annum, while loans were made at rates of 12—14 per cent per annum. Overhead costs were minimal; in 1470 the entire network only employed fifty-seven individuals, or from four to ten per branch.[3] On the asset side of the ledger, cash rarely exceeded 10 per cent of total assets, with loans or claims on other Medici branches representing the bulk of the remainder.

Lending policy was established and generally enforced by guidelines laid down by the family and its general manager in Florence. Newly appointed branch managers signed contracts which, for example, required them to lend only to reputable merchants or manufacturers. Princes, noblemen and the clergy were generally considered bad risks except possibly on a cash collateralised basis. The new London manager in 1446 agreed not to accept bribes or lend to himself or his family, to give preference to other Medici branches in sending bills and goods on consignment and to insure goods sent by sea. Credit limits were established for other Italian banks and for individual members of the clergy from cardinal to the Pope, but no credit was to be extended to bankers in Genoa, Venice, Brittany or Gascony. At year end the manager would take the branch books to Florence for a thorough audit. All hiring was controlled by Florence to prevent collusion.

During the first half century of operation, under the management of Giovanni de Medici through Cosimo de Medici, earnings were quite satisfactory. The bank as a whole made 10 per cent on its capital in its first year of operations. A study of a series of typical exchange transactions shows that a median interest return of 14 per cent on foreign currency loans was achieved.[4] Some branches were remarkably successful; Venice's annual earnings for several years averaged 60 per cent of the branch capital, while those of Geneva exceeded 30 per cent of capital throughout the second quarter of the fifteenth century.

In 1464, however, the Bank entered into a serious state of decline due to a combination of external political and economic events, serious loan losses stemming in large part from poor management in several branches, and increasingly ineffective control and direction from management in

Florence. Wars or other political conflicts involving Florence had serious repercussions on the viability of individual branches; French kings on several occasions forced the Lyons branch to close down or modify its policies, while Venice and Naples suffered from regional warfare. An imbalance of trade between Northern and Southern Europe severely restrained the financing of trade; exports from the north were dependent upon English wool, which was in short supply for economic reasons as well as English efforts to restrict the export of raw wool.

Loans to monarchs, often against the express policy of home office, produced massive losses, although in many branches the local ruler represented the only reasonably creditworthy borrower. The Milan branch was established as a gesture of support to the Duke of Milan, the Medici's political ally. Within eight years of its establishment, loans to the Duke and Duchess represented 37 per cent of total assets and 168 per cent of the branch's capital.[5] In London, loans to Edward IV represented the principal means of obtaining permission to export wool so as to provide remittances to cover English imports. Eventually over four times the branch's capital was lent to Edward, and the cost of borrowed funds to carry these non-accruing loans coupled with the periodic defaults stemming from the War of the Roses ate up the branch's profits. The Bruges manager far exceeded his established limit to Charles the Bold of Burgundy; over four times the branch's capital was outstanding to the Duke at the time of his death. Invariably these branch managers found themselves lending new funds to heads of state to recoup existing loans.

During the final years of the Medici Bank culminating in the expulsion of the Medici from Florence in 1494, the head office management under Lorenzo de Medici and his general manager, Sassetti, actively closed down unprofitable branches, mobilised cash resources and tried with limited success to control their branch managers. Loan losses of a multiple of capital in several branches, coupled with low cash reserves and the external political and economic factors mentioned above led, however, to the gradual liquidation of individual branches and the bank's ultimate demise. Even the once profitable Rome branch was liquidated after the Pope for political reasons repudiated his debts to the Medici and cancelled the alum contract. A recalcitrant manager in Lyons finally had to be jailed after losing a multiple of the branch's capital because of bad loans and stale merchandise stocks. Professor de Roover concludes that 'Techniques have changed, but human problems have remained the same. How to pick out the right person and put him in the right place was as much a problem for the Medici as it is in business today.'[6] With regard to lending policy, he notes that the 'congenital defect of . . . the financial type of sedentary merchant to drift from private banking into government finance'[7] made a major contribution to the Medici collapse.

The decline and fall of the Florentine merchant bankers was followed in the sixteenth century by a similar era of dominance by South German bankers led by the Fugger family as well as the development of sophisticated international money markets in centres such as Antwerp and Lyons.

Antwerp and other money centres were unregulated markets where private bankers traded commodities, engaged in money trading in the form of the purchase and sale of bills of exchange, and made short term direct loans to banks and governments. On the Antwerp Bourse loans of three to six months at interest rates of 8—12 per cent (depending on the credit) were made to banks like Fugger by other banks and wealthy individuals. Loans to governments, with or without guarantees by banks or well regarded subjects such as the City of Antwerp, were traded in the form of certificates at rates reflecting the borrower's credit record. In the 1540s and 1550s, the English government generally paid approximately 12 per cent per annum for its funds, while Spain would often pay a 16 per cent interest rate.[8] Rates paid would vary not only on the basis of the name of the royal borrower but also the quality of security or outside guarantee. Government loans syndicated among a number of Antwerp and Lyons banks of which one, the agent, held the collateral, were prevalent. In 1555, the French government issued the 'Grand Parti', a ten-year loan consolidating outstanding loans plus a certain amount of new money at a relatively high 16 per cent; the large number of individuals who rushed to participate in the loan were disappointed when the loan defaulted two years later.

The Fugger bank owes its ascent and collapse to the Habsburg family which it financed during the sixteenth and early seventeenth centuries. Direct loans to monarchs such as Maximilian and Charles V were initially made on a secured basis for a one-year maturity at a rate of 12—14 per cent per annum; these loans were financed by matching money market deposits on which interest at 8—10 per cent per annum was charged to Fugger as a prime borrowing name. Loans for purely political purposes were common; in 1530, to elect Charles V's brother as King of Rome, the Fugger made a 275,000 florin eight-year loan at 10 per cent interest secured by various official revenues with a front end fee of 40,000 florins, or 15 per cent of the principal amount, as a 'special refreshment and token of honor'.[9] Capital funds and deposits by the Fugger family usually represented the bulk of the balance sheet, with borrowings in the Antwerp Bourse representing the largest portion of external liabilities. In addition to loans, assets were made up of holdings of land, mines and commodities held for their own account.

Being imperial banker to an empire struggling to conquer the Low Countries and financed ultimately through precious metals from the New World was profitable but involved an increasing concentration of risk. In the seven years to 1546, for example, the Fugger bank earned an annual average of 19 per cent per annum on invested capital. On the other hand, direct and indirect loans to the Habsburg Emperor represented not only an increasing proportion of total assets but a substantial source of loan write-offs. In 1546, loans to the Emperor represented 2 million florins, or 28 per cent of total assets of 7.1 million florins and over half the entire loan portfolio; on the liability side, net worth represented 5.1 million florins and liabilities, mostly bills borrowed on the Antwerp market, 2 million florins.[10]

The bank increasingly found itself lending new funds to protect existing loans to the Habsburgs; collateral consisted of pledged tax receipts in the Netherlands or Spain which often were not forthcoming. Against a capital (reduced by loan losses) of 2 million florins, loans to the Hapsburgs rose to 4.5 million florins in 1563. After a series of agreed moratoria and official Spanish bankruptcies during which interest rates were reduced and maturities extended, about 8 million Rhenish gulders of Habsburg loans were finally written off in 1650, thereby wiping out most of the bank's earnings over the previous century.[11]

Merchant and Investment Banks During the Nineteenth Century

Between the Napoleonic wars and the late nineteenth century, international trade and investment flourished under the stimulus of capital exports and trade finance supplied by the London and Paris financial markets. Despite periodic economic crises during the period stemming from occasional commodity price collapses, over-extension of credit and financial panics, an apparently irresistible urge to invest European capital abroad brought forth waves of new financial institutions. Most of these new banks collapsed in the wake of the century's recurrent slumps and panics, but a number survived to become some of today's leading financial institutions. In the analysis which follows, particular attention will be placed on the qualities which appear to differentiate the new international banks which survived from those which disappeared.

The new international banks in the nineteenth century were engaged in two fundamentally different activities: investment banking, or the arrangement on an agency or underwriting basis of long-term funds for infrastructural and industrial development, and trade financing on the traditional basis of the bill drawn, usually on London, to finance commodity exports and imports. Both sectors had their share of casualties.

Typical of the trade financing, or commercial lending, enterprises was that of Baring Brothers' activities in financing US trade with England.[12] On the strength of its close correspondent ties in America and the relative cheapness of the London money market, Barings offered lines of credit to American commodity exporters and commercial houses interested in drawing sterling bills on London to finance trade or to deal in foreign exchange. As London correspondent of the Bank of the United States, it functioned for a certain period as the semi-official London banker to the US government. With interest rates in the early 1830s of 5½–7 per cent per annum in the US and 2¾–3¾ per cent in London, the latter naturally was an attractive financing market, and the United States soon became the most highly regarded credit risk outside England in the 1830s.

From a limited capital base of £492,000 in 1830, Barings operated profitably throughout the century with a minimal loss record despite the series of public and private defaults, bank failures and commodity price collapses which marked the period. Supported by good economic intelligence and credit files contained in its 'Private Remarks Book', Barings was able to contract its outstanding short-term bill obligations or insist on additional security when it sensed an approaching crisis. Clean advances were made against the shipment of commodities with an appropriate margin; only second-line credits, which were in the minority, required additional security in the form of documents. Consignment business was emphasised; Barings charged 2½ per cent to sell consigned merchandise and 1 per cent as agent to market US securities. No loans in excess of the borrower's capital were permitted, and the bank generally required that all of a customer's financing be done through Barings. Interest on outstandings was usually debited at a rate of 5 per cent, while credit balances with Barings generally earned 4 per cent enterest.[13] Of all the major Anglo-American financing houses, only Barings survived the 1837 crisis and commodity price collapse without assistance from the Bank of England.

Whereas Barings operated only through a representative in the United States, a number of British-owned banks were established with a network of foreign branches to exploit trade with particular commodity-rich areas such as Latin America and South Africa. Control of these banks was exerted through a board of senior management in London, where the money market was used as a source of short-term finance to cover the debit balances of the overseas branches.

In Latin America, the predecessors of the Bank of London and South America survived the sharp commodity price fluctuations, public and private defaults and civil strife of the mid-nineteenth century.[14] Managers of BOLSA branches were instructed to finance only short-term trade movements which were self-liquidating in nature, not crops in the ground. Loans to governments or against mortgages or other securities were generally prohibited. Loans and deposits were matched on a currency basis despite the temptation to convert sterling deposits and lend the higher yielding local currencies, and liquidity in the form of cash normally represented one-third of the branches' deposits. In South Africa, the Standard Bank from its establishment in 1863 also concentrated on commodity financing despite the attractions of other forms of lending.[15] Wool, gold and diamond exports were financed, despite some losses due to the collapse of prices in the 1860s and 1880s. While some losses were suffered on loans against mining shares and claims, the general policy of lending against the commodities themselves was a major factor in the survival of the bank.

A unique phenomenon of the nineteenth century was the development of investment banking institutions such as the Rothschild bank, the Crédit Mobilier and geographically specialised banks whose principal activity was the intermediation of long-term capital exports from England and France. Undeterred by depressingly regular defaults by private and public overseas borrowers, the British and French public through their bankers financed a world-wide programme of infrastructure and industry — railroads, canals, public utilities, mines and factories — through term debt and equity issues floated in London and Paris. The banks either placed the funds as agent or on an underwriting basis. Issues were priced at a discount from par with the underwriter seeking to obtain the major portion of his compensation from an increase over the offering price. In many cases, banks promoted new overseas ventures, retained an equity stake and maintained a market in the venture's publicly-held securities.

Among the more successful investment banks of the period, the Rothschilds operated throughout most of the nineteenth century as a single firm with branches in Paris, London, Vienna and Frankfurt, each managed by a member of the family. Close political connections with the rulers of the time were utilised to prevent wars which could jeopardise their various interests; Prince Metternich's right-hand man in the early part of the century, Frederick von Gentz, was actually a salaried employee of the Rothschilds.[16] The bank initiated the Continental railroad building boom in 1835 by obtaining the Nordbahn concession from the Austrian government. In Spain, to obtain the European quicksilver monopoly, they bid in 1835 for the same concession owned in the sixteenth century by the Fugger; the bid succeeded at least in part because of a simultaneous loan and gifts to the financially hard-pressed Spanish government.[17] Political as well as economic conditions were attached to the loans which were granted to virtually all major European countries; a railroad credit to King Leopold of Belgium in 1837 was granted on the condition, among others, that he suppress a potential revolutionary movement in Luxembourg, and that no further disbursements should take place if war were to break

bilier for control of a European railroad
mpaign of bids and takeovers which
btaining control of the northern Italian
ian war of independence against Austria.
ted by gains on the sale of stock of the
fees earned through the flotation of
suffered on securities held during the
iod must have been substantial.
y the Pereire brothers and the Fould
ed the first institutional attempt to tap
ough a joint-stock company for capital
work of affiliated investment banks was
Financial Society Limited), Spain
ny (Darmstadter Bank), Italy (Credito

Mobiliare Italiano), and Holland (Crédit Neerlandais). Activity was directed initially toward the promotion, construction and acquisition of railroads financed by Crédit Mobilier bond issues, usually in competition with the Rothschild bank. Imitators of the Crédit Mobilier sprang up throughout Europe; four were established in Spain alone in the 1850s, with the result that 80 per cent of railway trackage in Spain in 1861 belonged to French-controlled companies.[20] In practice, the Crédit Mobilier was prepared to lend for a longer period against riskier securities than would be accepted by a commercial bank.

Earnings were derived primarily from the promotion of new ventures, generally through the sale of shares sold at a premium after the initial offering. While it contributed 40 per cent of the 650 million francs total capital of the foreign banks it helped found, its own capital for most of the fifteen years of its life did not exceed a fairly modest sixty million francs.[21] While its flexibility and aggressiveness created a number of highly successful financial institutions and projects, it suffered heavy losses as the result of the collapse of its Dutch bank and its railroads in Russia and Switzerland. A loan to finance Maximilian's expedition to Mexico may also have contributed to the Crédit Mobilier's demise in 1867, when the Pereire brothers left the bank and its various emanations were liquidated or acquired by outside interests. In retrospect, inadequate project analysis, which led to substantial cost overruns and inadequate revenues for the projects financed by the Crédit Mobilier, also was a factor in its disappearance.

Such was the unprecedented enthusiasm on the part of British and French individual investors for the higher yields and glamour of foreign securities that 'Any government which claimed sovereignty over a bit of the earth's surface and a fraction of its inhabitants could find a financial agent in London and purchasers for her bonds.'[22]

With foreign government and infrastructure or railway bonds effectively yielding 5½–8 per cent per annum compared to British Consols at 3–4 per cent, the supply of funds was vast and the borrowers responded enthusiastically. Investment banks in London and Paris and the newly-formed overseas banks would compete vigorously for an exclusive mandate to raise funds for a given government or to establish a railway or mineral concession. With such a mandate usually came the profitable remittance, cash management and agency business for that borrower. Either on a best efforts or underwritten basis, the issue would be placed with individual investors in Europe through the major clearing and deposit banks in England, France and Germany. In the 1820s, management or underwriting fees amounted to 2–5 per cent of the nominal amount of the loan (usually far in excess of the issue price) and additional profits were earned by agency fees, the use of free balances and the manipulation of the market price by placing forward purchase orders to insure an opening premium over the offering price.[23] For the latter purpose, the proceeds of the loan itself were often used to create a premium which would attract additional buyers. Bonds were often allocated to banks at a price below the price to the public as a form of compensation.

The peak of the foreign-bond mania and the banking expansion which accompanied it was reached in the late 1870s. 'No country was so willing as England to expand credit beyond the limits of commercial prudence.'[24] Not only were less developed countries (Russia, Turkey, Spain, Egypt, a host of Latin American countries) and high risk start-up projects (a variety of US, Latin American and European railways) financed, but lack of due diligence brought to the market a number of fraudulent or imaginary offerings. Gregor MacGregor, a Scottish adventurer, persuaded a London house whose principal was a former Lord Mayor of London to bring to market a £200,000 loan to the State of Poyais, an imaginary state on the Mosquito Coast of Nicaragua, which was convertible into freehold land in 'Poyais'.[25] Notwithstanding the death of colonists who unwittingly set out for Poyais, MacGregor was able two years later to perform the same feat with another London house for another imaginary kingdom. The railway boom was such that a promotion in the US by the name of the Atlantic and Great Western Railroad, which was to run between the metropoli of Salamanca, New York and Dayton, Ohio, was able in 1865 to borrow its entire capitalisation, including rolled up interest, in the London market without a penny of equity invested.[26]

The default record on these borrowings, while painful, did not deter individual European investors for long. In 1841–2 nine US states suspended interest payments, and in subsequent years approximately one-half of the US railroads went into receivership. In 1873–4 alone, the governments of Honduras, Costa Rica, Santo Domingo, Paraguay, Spain, Egypt, Turkey, Peru, Uruguay, Liberia, Guatemala and Bolivia defaulted, often because the fear generated by the contemporary wave of defaults prevented otherwise creditworthy countries from refinancing existing obligations.[27]

The premium yield on overseas securities and the enthusiasm for commodity wealth abroad led to the establishment at mid-century of dozens of banks specialising in exporting British and French funds to specific less developed regions with apparent economic potential. Apart from the banks discussed above, the Near and Far East as well as Europe and North and South America attracted banks promoted and often controlled by London and Parisian financial groups. Most of these promotions either never opened their doors or closed within a few years due to massive loan losses.

The end of the Crimean War and the obvious capital requirements of the Turkish Empire led to the establishment of promotions such as the Bank of Egypt in 1855, which was sponsored by some leading London bankers and was the first British joint stock bank to commence business abroad.[28] Operating with branches in Egypt and a head office in London, its management guidelines forbade land speculation, placed a ceiling on loans to directors of one-third of the total and limited the issue of its notes to three times capital plus the bullion reserve. As in the case of most banks of its kind, however, its loan portfolio was tied to the fortunes of the Egyptian economy — primarily cotton — and the creditworthiness of the local ruler. Following some early losses and the ejection of the individual who had promoted and managed the bank, it paid a dividend of 10—20 per cent on its capital through the 1860s and 1870s but finally collapsed following the 1907 crisis when half of its acceptance liabilities proved uncollectable.

The Anglo-Egyptian Bank, a competitor established in 1864 by two major British banks, was rescued by the Egyptian Viceroy himself, who voluntarily took up half of the bank's share of a sticky government loan underwritten by Anglo-Egyptian and made an *ex gratia* payment to compensate the bank for its loss on the remainder.[29]

The capital requirements of Turkey itself attracted a variety of new institutions promoted by British and French banks, of which the Imperial Ottoman Bank was the principal survivor. With British investors owning over half the issued capital, the bank assumed quasi-central banking status through the issue of notes and collection of tax revenues. Substantial earnings were realised on foreign exchange dealings, and the bank not only survived the Turkish government's defaults in the 1870s but was usually able to pay a 12 per cent dividend on capital funds.

In North America, a total of five British-owned banks were operating in California alone in the 1860s; activities included dealing in bullion, advances on merchandise and securities and the sale of sterling bills. One of these banks, the London and San Francisco Bank, was owned by ten British and ten German banks and was finally acquired in 1905 by the Bank of California.

In the Far East, the scene of an active three-cornered trade among China, India and England, a grand total of twenty-two newly established Anglo-Eastern banks on the brink of liquidation were dealt a final blow as the result of the 1866 financial crisis associated with the crash of Overend Gurney.[30] The first British-owned bank in the Far East, the Oriental Banking Corporation, survived the 1866 crisis but was liquidated towards the end of the century following the collapse of silver prices on which the Far Eastern economy was based. The principal survivor of these banks was the Hong Kong and Shanghai Banking Corporation, which survived not only the 1866 crash, civil strife in China, bad debts in Hong Kong but also losses in the London office through the unauthorised purchase of US bonds. Loans were generally made in silver and tied to foreign trade, and substantial foreign exchange profits were realised.

Towards the end of the century the British and French overseas banks were joined by offshore subsidiaries established by the major German mixed banks. The 1870s saw the establishment in London of banks such as the London and Hanseatic Bank (Commerzbank) and German Bank of London (Deutsche Bank).

In Europe itself, a host of consortium institutions had a brief but eventful life in the 1860s. The Anglo-Italian Bank was set up by such leading English bankers as George Peabody & Co. in 1864 to introduce English banking techniques to Italy. While the directors believed that 'by lending money to public establishments for a longer period than was usual in [England] and making advances to municipalities on the security of the rates, [the Directors] had reason to believe a safe and profitable business might be secured.'[31] Within a few years, exhange losses resulted in the write-off of over half the bank's capital. The English and Swedish Bank, run by English bankers, survivied three years; the Madrid Bank in Spain lasted two years before being wound up. At least three British-owned banks set up in Russia had disappeared by 1871.

To the normal risks of war and political conflict, violent fluctuations of commodity prices and mal-adminstration of less developed economies and political systems was thus added in the nineteenth century an overwhelming and relentless appetite for foreign securities which was sustained, if not whetted, by the activities of individual promoters and newly established specialist international banks. While it is difficult to generalise on the basis of available information, it would appear that the demise of so many new institutions is attributable as much to poor and inexperienced management in the form of over-concentration of credit, mismatching of lending and borrowing currencies, lack of analysis and overenthusiasm in a complex environment as to the external factors mentioned. There would also appear to have been a greater mortality rate among overseas subsidiary banks which were less tightly controlled from home office than branches. In any case, over half the new international banks promoted between 1856 and 1865 aborted, and over a quarter of the promotions which were actually set up were insolvent within five years.[32]

Despite these disappointments, about £3.8 billion in foreign long term publicly issued capital was held by British investors in 1913; this represented about 25 per cent of Britain's Gross National Product and roughly 10 per cent of the country's net income.[33] While the proportion of French GNP invested abroad was somewhat less, a total of 109 foreign securities were quoted in 1869 on the Paris Bourse. Thanks in large part to the efforts of the international investment banks, Latin American owed foreign investors about $6,000 million by 1913, and Russia had become the largest European borrower on the eve of the Revolution.[34]

US Commercial Bank Expansion in the Early Twentieth Century
One of the most interesting episodes of the development of international banking is the burst of expansion abroad by American commercial banks during the period beginning with World War I and continuing during the 1920s. As in the case of so many other banks before them who moved quickly into new markets with significant political and economical risks, mistakes were made and substantial write-offs of loans and equity

investments affected American bank profit and loss statements in the 1920s and 1930s.

Until 1913 international banking had been dominated by the European-controlled overseas or colonial banks as a consequence of the export of European capital in the nineteenth century. In 1910, for example, there were thirty-two British colonial banks headquartered in London with 2104 branches in the colonies in addition to eighteen other British-owned foreign banks with 175 branches.[35] Eighteen French colonial banks had 104 offices, and German and Dutch banks operated somewhat smaller networks.

The passage of the Federal Reserve Act in 1913, coupled with the outbreak of World War I which was to turn the United States from the world's largest debtor nation into a major creditor, precipitated a rapid expansion of foreign branches and subsidiaries of American banks. While a few consortium-owned subsidiary banks had been established under state laws in earlier years, the Federal Reserve Act permitted national banks to branch abroad and to accept drafts for the first time. The dollar acceptance thus came to play a major role at the expense of the sterling draft drawn on a country which had been hard hit by the war and whose post war balance of payments vulnerability was to severely restrict its former role as the world's banker.

US banks moved abroad initially through branches or subsidiaries which themselves branched abroad. Six consortium subsidiaries were incorporated under state law and included:

(1) American Foreign Banking Corporation, which was incorporated in 1917 by over thirty banks in America and Canada, established seventeen foreign branches in Latin America and Europe. The Chase Bank, which was one of the stockholders, acquired its three remaining branches in 1925.

(2) Asia Banking Corporation, incorporated in 1918 and owned by the Guaranty Trust Company, Continental Bank of Chicago and other US banks, opened eleven foreign branches in the Far East and San Francisco. Following a voluntary liquidation in 1924, its remaining assets were bought up by a subsidiary of the National City Bank.

(3) Mercantile Bank of the Americas, which was established in 1915 with a capital of $11 million by Brown Brothers, Guaranty Trust and other US interests; it rapidly opened branches in Europe and established controlled subsidiaries in Peru, Venezuela, Columbia, Brazil, Cuba, Costa Rica, Nicaragua and Honduras. At its zenith the bank had forty five overseas offices. The collapse of commodity prices in 1920 forced a reorganisation of the bank in 1922 as the Bank of Central and South America; the bank's Havana office alone lent $25 million against sugar which dropped in price from $.21 to $.02 per pound. Despite the stockholder support of banks such as J. P.

Morgan, Guaranty Trust, Seligman, Corn Exchange and W. R. Grace, the new bank, which operated twenty-two foreign offices, was sold three years later to the Royal Bank of Canada.

(4) Park-Union Foreign Banking Corporation was set up in 1919 by the National Park Bank of New York and the Union Bank of Canada to finance trade with the Far East through branches in Japan, China and Paris. It went into voluntary liquidation in 1922.

At their zenith, the foreign banking subsidiaries operated eighty-one overseas branches.[36] By 1927, however, all the remaining consortium-owned foreign banking subsidiaries had been absorbed by US banks. Companies established under the new Edge Act, passed in 1919, fared no better. All three formed in the early 1920s, including one consortium with 1000 banking stockholders, disappeared by 1933. Of the eighteen banking corporations — Edge Act and Agreement — which initially came under the Federal Reserve's jurisdiction, only three survived beyond the early 1930s.

The failure of these new ventures sponsored by major US banking institutions has been attributed to a combination of inexperienced management, over-rapid expansion, the 1920 foreign trade crisis, excessive eagerness and competition for business, conflicts among the banking stockholders and the usual problems of doing business in countries with a significant degree of political instability and vulnerability to commodity price fluctuation. In several cases parent banks began to perform the same functions as their subsidiaries. While the consortium approach clearly limited the exposure of individual banks, 'it soon appeared that the bank stockholders in such institutions were inclined to suspect one another or to fear that through some lack of loyalty one or the other of them would be disadvantaged'.[37] The lack of experience of American bankers was blamed:

> the expansion was unduly rapid and unwarranted; trained men for the management of foreign banks were lacking . . . It is by this long drawn out method that British and Canadian banks have built up the personnel of their foreign branches, and there seems to be no shorter road to real success in overseas banking.[38]

The ultimate fate of the early consortium banks was liquidation, absorption of assets by one or more of the stockholders, or sale of assets to another bank.

Branch banking by organisations such as National City Bank, Chase, Morgan, and First of Boston produced more positive results in Latin America, Asia and Europe. From a total of twenty-six foreign offices in 1916, the total (including branches of subsidiaries) rose to 181 in 1920, although it fell back in 1926 to 107 primarily as a result of the liquidation of subsidiary banks. The National City Bank alone in 1926 had a world-wide network of fifty-one direct branches in addition to the twenty-two branches of its wholly-owned subsidiary.

US corporate investment and commodity imports encouraged the establishment of a number of US branches throughout Latin America, although the periodic collapse of commodity prices caused many sleepless nights for bankers. With an estimated $1200 million lent to Latin American borrowers by 1929, the price collapse of 1930 and subsequent widespread defaults had a significant impact on American banks. The drop in sugar prices in 1921 from 22 cents to 3.5 cents per pound resulted in US banks taking over and running Cuban plantations and mills as well as writing off substantial loans. When commodity prices dropped again in 1930, the banks were better prepared and had begun to insist on such safeguards as earlier repayment and prior sale of sugar to an ultimate buyer or on the futures market. Throughout the inter-war period, support to South American countries in payments difficulties was provided by guarantees from the US Export-Import Bank. American bankers in Latin America were accused of lack of sound banking judgement, overexpansion, cutting lending rates and lack of understanding of the nature of one or two crop economies.

Other branches were located in London and Paris to perform securities arbitrage, handle foreign exchange transactions and service US corporations in Europe. In Asia, the branches of US banks with their more conservative policies succeeded where the consortium banks had failed; profits were made on immigrant remittances, loans against gold and silver, and trade financing.

Somewhat chastened by their mixed experience in Latin America, US banks turned to European borrowers which traditionally had enjoyed the best credit ratings. The ravages of the war and subsequent inflation had, however, somewhat damaged these ratings. The onslaught of foreign banks continued during the 1920s:

> Not only American and English but also Dutch, Swiss, Swedish and French banks and issuing houses approached foreign states, cities, railroads, public utilities and industrial corporations, offering them loans and credits without serious concern as to their ability to repay in the lender's currency.[39]

The lack of any international co-ordination in lending to Central European countries, the collapse of the New York Stock Exchange and the consequent check to the outflow of loan funds and the tariff barriers placed on European exports finally culminated in 1931 in the collapse of key Central European banks and the standstill agreement on German short term debt to foreign creditors. Germany had enjoyed a top credit rating before the war, and the US bankers were attracted by the higher rates paid by German banks and corporations on short-term, presumably self-liquidating, acceptance financing. As a partner in Kuhn Loeb put it during a 1931 Senate investigation,

> England . . . had an age-old prestige for judgement and wisdom in the matter of international financial borrowings. We were perfectly justified in following . . . the example of a wise old nation like England, being right there, and a wise old nation like Holland . . . who, in proportion to their resources, gave larger short term credits to Germany than America did . . . It may be locked up for a while, yes, but that is the ordinary risk of business.[40]

In total, Germany owed its foreign bank creditors an estimated $1000 million, of which US banks held about $600 million in short term credits. One US bank was reported to have had $130 million outstanding to Germany in 1931. When US banks began in March 1931 to pull back their short term credits to foreigners, roughly 40 per cent of US short term claims were on German borrowers. According to Thomas Lamont's testimony before the Senate, about ninety US banks were lending to Germany; as of November 1932, about $500 million in short term credit was held by thirty New York banks and twenty-eight interior banks.[41] Standstill agreements under which US banks agreed to maintain outstanding credit were extended on an annual basis until World War II; from time to time portions of the dollar debt were converted into marks which could be sold at a discount, used to acquire German assets or held in blocked accounts. The steady depreciation of the mark, however, ultimately resulted in substantial write-offs on the books of American banks. Similar standstill agreements for smaller amounts of bank loans were agreed with Austria and Hungary.

By the end of 1933, when hundreds of banks around the world had closed their doors permanently, 67 per cent of the Latin American and 46 per cent of the European-issued dollar bonds were in default as to interest. A US government report summed up the overseas lending activities in the 1920s as follows:

> Under the high pressure salesmanship methods by which foreign issues were solicited and sold, our loans proved to be their undoing. The flotation of one loan frequently came to be regarded as adequate justification for further issues to the same borrower or the same country without regard to the growing burden of indebtedness.[42]

2 The Evolution and Description of the Euro-Bank

As has happened so often in the history of international banking, a massive and sustained growth in overseas trade and investment has brought forth a new generation of international financial institutions during the past decade. The thirty years since the end of World War II have witnessed an unprecedented internationalisation of the world's economies in the context of an equally remarkable rate of overall economic growth. What has particularly marked this post-war period of international banking growth has been the evolution of a network of sophisticated markets in foreign currency loans and deposits with an ease of access that has permitted the emergence of new banking institutions which otherwise might not have seen the light of day.

It is this new generation of banks which is the subject of this book. The significance of the Euro-bank lies less in its physical importance than in the fact that it approximates a 'pure' international bank in microcosm without the domestic base which characterises other institutions whose international activity may be much larger in absolute terms. Recognising that any definition in such a large and varied banking community as the Eurocurrency market must necessarily be imprecise, I have defined a Euro-bank to be an international banking institution with its own capital base, a certain degree of management autonomy, executive offices in London or another international finance centre, and whose principal activity is related directly or indirectly to the taking of deposits in Eurocurrencies (currencies held outside their national market) and on-lending them to customers or other banks. A large number of Euro-banks also participate actively in various aspects of the Eurobond market. While a number of common characteristics exist between Euro-banks and overseas branches of American and other national banks, the former usually develop a special identity because of factors such as their separate management structure, own capitalisation and need to attract funds under their own name.

In most cases, these banks have been established by other financial institutions since the mid-1960s specifically to operate in the Euro-currency and Eurobond markets. Ownership structures range from the wholly-owned subsidiary to consortium banks with a dozen or more stockholders and publicly quoted institutions. While their objectives, sponsorship, structures and size may vary significantly, they generally derive most of their earnings from interest income and fund themselves primarily in the interbank market. Their principal centre of operations tends to be in one of the international money market centres such as London, Luxembourg or Singapore, although for tax or administrative reasons they may be incorporated elsewhere. For analytical purposes in later chapters I have focused on London-based Euro-banks in view of their relative importance in size and number, the availability of published information and the dominance of London as the principal international financial market, but the management issues discussed should be equally relevant to Euro-banks in centres such as Singapore, Luxembourg or Hong Kong.

The history, structure, theory and practice of the Euro-markets have been described in some detail in a number of excellent volumes and articles, and the purpose of this book is not to duplicate what has already been written on these subjects. A few brief paragraphs on the nature and structure of the Eurocurrency market, however, may provide a useful introduction to a discussion of the Euro-banks themselves.

The market for Eurocurrencies (defined as dollars and other leading currencies deposited in banks other than those of the country where these currencies are issued) grew up in the late 1950s and 1960s primarily in response to the rapid and sustained expansion of international trade and investment, the large US balance of payments deficits which financed a good portion of this expansion, and various national — principally American — exchange, interest rate and reserve requirement regulations which encouraged the development of an unregulated international money market where funds could flow freely in response to supply and demand. As measured by the Bank for International Settlements (BIS), which includes the outstanding amount of foreign currency credits channeled through the nine European countries covered by its statistics but excludes interbank lending within a given country and lending to local institutions, the Eurocurrency market grew at an amazing compound annual rate of 31 per cent between 1969 and 1974 to reach a gross level at December 1974 of $214,000 million in assets.[1]

Approximately 25 per cent of these funds were on-lent to non-bank customers, and at end 1974 the dollar component of these assets was 73 per cent of the total. If one were to include non-European markets such as the Bahamas, Panama, Tokyo, Canada and Singapore, the size of the world Eurocurrency market at end-1974 (including domestic interbank and other lending of foreign currencies) has been estimated by Morgan Guaranty Trust Company to be approximately $370,000 million and by Bankers Trust Company to be roughly $380,000 million.[2] During 1975, these sources report a continuation of this growth trend.

Table A shows an estimated breakdown of the gross market by David

Ashby of Bankers Trust Company published in the *Banker* in 1974 and updated to include end-1974 figures. While no direct comparison with national markets is possible, it is interesting to note that at end-1974 the total money supply of the United States on a comparable basis (M2 plus large C/Ds) represented $707,000 million.

In achieving this impressive year to year growth, which was only interrupted briefly in mid-1974, the market has consistently confounded observers who predicted its demise because of such concerns as lack of confidence, the opening up of the US market in 1974 when exchange controls were lifted, the by-passing of the market by OPEC funds, and the drying up of the supply of funds. Innovation and flexibility have characterised the Eurocurrency market, which has developed new loan pricing techniques, tapped new sources of funds, located new borrowers and developed loan syndication techniques which did not exist only ten years ago.

While the market originated and is still centred in London, satellite markets throughout the world have grown up where foreign currency deposits are traded among banks. According to the Bankers Trust data, the London market (including the interbank portion) comprises somewhat over one-third of the world-wide market. American banks, which represent the biggest factor in the Eurocurrency market, hold about half of their foreign branch deposits in London (46 per cent in December 1974),[3] while the United Kingdom represents a bit less than one half of the foreign currency assets in the reporting BIS countries. Large amounts of Euro-currencies are held by banks in the Bahamas and Caymans, Belgium — Luxembourg, France, Italy, Switzerland, Canada, Japan and Singapore as indicated in Table A. In addition, the London interbank market as well as other European domestic markets represent a significant volume of foreign currencies traded. In recent years non-European markets such as the Bahamas and Singapore have grown more rapidly than the traditional European centres.

One of the most significant aspects of the market growth has been the entry of new and existing banks into the various Euromarkets. At end-1974 a total of 335 different banks from fifty-three countries were represented in London either directly or through an equity interest in a London-based consortium bank; this figure includes ninety-seven of the 100 largest banks in the world as measured by the *Banker*.[4] In terms of banks actually dealing in the Eurocurrency market, a total of 253 banks as of September 1975 were authorised by the Bank of England to deal in foreign currencies and thereby participate in the Euro-market; as of May 1975, 352 banks were listed in Bank of England statistics on foreign currency activities of banks in the United Kingdom. Table B provides a recent breakdown of foreign currency assets and liabilities by category of bank in the London markets.

The largest single component within the overall UK foreign currency

TABLE A

ESTIMATED SIZE OF TOTAL GROSS EUROCURRENCY MARKET
(amounts in $1000m., end-year)

	1972 Amount	% of Total[c]	1973 Amount	% of Total[c]	1974 Amount	% of Total[c]
1. Europe—based Market						
A. Commercial Banks' External Assets (a)	132	62	188	59	214	56
of which:						
Belgium—Luxembourg	(14)	(6)	(24)	(8)	(32)	(8)
France	(16)	(7)	(28)	(9)	(32)	(8)
Germany	(3)	(1)	(7)	(2)	(8)	(2)
Italy	(19)	(9)	(24)	(8)	(13)	(3)
Netherlands	(6)	(3)	(9)	(3)	(12)	(3)
Sweden	(1)	(1)	(2)	(1)	(2)	(1)
Switzerland	(16)	(8)	(10)	(3)	(12)	(3)
United Kigdom	(56)	(26)	(84)	(26)	(103)	(27)
B. London Interbank Market[b]	21	10	34	11	36	9
C. Other UK Domestic Market[b]	5	2	10	3	15	4
D. Other European Domestic Market[b]	14	7	20	6	27	7
E. Sub-Total: Gross Europe-based Market	127	81	252	79	292	77
2. Non-European Market						
F. Bahamas and Grand Cayman[b]	18	8	33	10	44	12
G. Canada[a]	8	4	12	4	14	4
H. Japan[a]	10	5	16	5	19	5
I. Panama[b]	1	1	2	1	4	1
J. Singapore[b]	3	1	6	2	10	3
3. Grand Total Gross Market (A through J)	212	100	321	100	383	100

[a]Source: Bank for International Settlements.
[b]Source: Bankers Trust Company — David Ashby.
[c]Totals may not add due to rounding

TABLE B

BREAKDOWN OF FOREIGN CURRENCY ASSETS AND LIABILITIES OF UK BANKS AS OF 16 JULY 1975
(amounts in £1000m.)

ASSETS

| | Total Non-Sterling Assets | | of which: | | | | | | | |
| | | | Loans to UK Banks | | C/Ds | | UK Borrowers | | Overseas Borrowers | |
	Amount	% of Total Banks	Amount	% of Total	Amount	% of Total	Amount	% of Total	Amount	% of Total
All Banks	76.6	100	17.4	23	1.5	2	7.4	10	49.3	64
of which:										
(a) London Clearing Banks	4.0	5	1.2	30	—	—	.9	23	1.8	45
(b) Accepting Houses	2.7	4	.5	19	.2	7	.4	15	1.5	56
(c) American Banks	28.9	38	6.9	24	.4	1	2.3	8	19.2	66
(d) Japanese Banks	10.5	14	1.0	10	—	—	.5	5	9.0	86
(e) Consortium Banks	4.7	6	.8	17	.2	4	.4	9	3.3	70
(f) Other Overseas Banks	16.9	22	5.1	30	.5	3	1.4	8	9.7	57

LIABILITIES

| | Total Non-Sterling Liabilities | | of which: | | | | | |
| | | | Deposits from UK Banking Sector | | Overseas Deposits | | C/Ds | |
	Amount	% of Total Banks	Amount	% of Total	Amount	% of Total	Amount	% of Total
All Banks	76.3	100	17.2	23	51.7	68	5.4	7
of which:								
(a) London Clearing Banks	3.9	5	.8	21	2.5	64	.3	8
(b) Accepting Houses	2.7	4	.8	30	1.7	63	.1	4
(c) American Banks	29.2	38	5.3	18	20.0	68	3.0	10
(d) Japanese Banks	10.5	14	3.0	29	7.3	70	.2	2
(e) Consortium Banks	4.5	6	1.6	36	2.8	62	.1	2
(f) Other Overseas Banks	16.9	22	3.5	21	12.2	72	.9	5

Source: *Bank of England Quarterly Bulletin*, vol. 15, no. 3 (Sep 1975).

market statistics is branches and subsidiaries of American banks, which reflects the importance of the dollar segment of the market and the relative priority given to international operations by these banks. A recent US Treasury study estimates that US banks represented at end-1974 about 53 per cent of outstanding foreign non-bank claims of banks on a world-wide basis.[5] While their share of the London market has dropped from 50 per cent in 1970 to 38 per cent at mid-1975, much of this decline reflects transfers of funds to tax haven branches for internal reasons. A total of fifty-seven US banks in London in mid-1975 thus had total sterling and foreign currency liabilities and capital funds in excess of the combined balance sheets of the UK clearing banks. Japanese banks represent about 14 per cent of the London Eurocurrency market, while other overseas banks account for 22 per cent.

Table B also points up the importance for London banks of overseas business; roughly two-thirds of their foreign currency liabilities and assets relate to non-UK residents. Japanese and consortium banks tend to have the highest concentration of assets in loans to overseas borrowers with the UK clearing banks and accepting houses naturally lending a relatively high proportion of assets to UK borrowers. Consortium and Japanese banks and Accepting Houses are also the largest net takers from the London interbank market on a relative basis; 36 per cent of the former's foreign currency liabilities are derived from the interbank market while only 17 per cent of assets are re-lent to the market. Certificates of deposit, which represent 7 per cent of total liabilities — with the US banks accounting for the bulk of the market — total only 2 per cent of foreign currency assets of London banks. London banks as a whole in mid-1975 were holding 23 per cent of their foreign currency assets in London interbank deposits, although Japanese and consortium banks showed significantly smaller percentages. Local UK customer business represented only 5—10 per cent of total non-sterling assets for the categories of American, Japanese, consortium and other overseas banks.

The importance of London in terms of numbers of banks is shown by Table C, which provides a breakdown as of September 1975 by type of banking vehicle for thirty-two financial centres. With a total number of 449 vehicles ranging from representative offices to consortium banks, London has more than twice the number of vehicles as New York with 179 and Hong Kong with 149. Within the overall London total are eighty-six consortium affiliates and sixty-one subsidiaries, within which categories are to be found the Euro-banks which are the focus of this book.

The Euro-bank which is the subject of this book does not represent a significant share of the market in terms of individual or collective size. While it is difficult — and not particularly relevant — to quantify the importance of separately capitalised banks which make up this category, a few unrelated numbers may be useful. Consortium banks in London,

TABLE C

LEAGUE TABLE OF WORLD FINANCIAL CENTRES — SEPTEMBER 1975

Centre	Rep. Office	Subsidiary	Branch	Multi-National Consortium Affiliate	Total
London	93	61	209	86	449
New York	66	41	63	9	179
Hong Kong	54	43	33	19	149
Singapore	40	13	47	11	111
Sao Paulo	59	21	12	10	102
Nassau	—	26	65	5	96
Tokyo	52	4	40	—	96
Frankfurt	50	9	32	4	95
Sydney	49	9	4	25	87
Beirut	52	15	16	3	86
Brussels	20	21	21	12	74
Mexico City	62	5	2	2	71
Luxembourg	2	37	11	9	59
Rio de Janeiro	31	13	8	3	55
Buenos Aires	38	5	13	2	58
Djakarta	32	1	11	8	52
Geneva	4	23	9	10	46
Zurich	17	13	8	5	43
Los Angeles	8	13	21	2	44
Chicago	14	4	20	6	44
Johannesburg	23	12	—	6	41
Caracas	36	1	3	1	41
Kuala Lumpur	9	6	15	10	40
San Francisco	5	13	20	2	40
Madrid	34	4	3	1	42
Melbourne	13	5	6	17	41
Tehran	33	3	1	2	39
Panama	6	14	15	3	38
Bogota	22	7	3	1	33
Manila	19	1	4	7	31
Milan	14	7	10	—	31
Bangkok	4	8	8	8	28

Source: *Who is Where*, published by the Banker Research Unit.

which represent a major segment of the Euro-bank sector, had total liabilities and capital in July, 1975 of £5,500 million, or 4 per cent of the UK banking sector total of £131,500 million.[6] At the close of their 1974 fiscal year, the forty consortium and subsidiary banks in my statistical sample of London Euro-banks had capital funds of £434 million and total assets of £6,700 million. Recognising the importance of the American-owned banks in the Eurocurrency market, it may be useful to note that 125 US banks operated abroad at the end of 1973 through seventy-eight controlled subsidiaries to complement their overseas branch network of 694 offices; most of these subsidiaries are designed to complement the commercial banking activities of the parent.[7] The *Banker* lists a total of fifty 'Eurocurrency Banks' in November 1974 in London, using a categorisation which roughly corresponds to my own of Euro-bank.[8]

London has attracted by far the largest number of Euro-banks in large part because of the size, sophistication and breadth of the interbank deposit market which is essential to these relatively new banks as a source of deposits. Other advantages include a flexible regulatory mechanism which has proven forceful enough to restore calm during the 1974 crisis of confidence, excellent communications, the attraction of London as a residence for senior executives, and the infrastructure and international banking traditions which London has established over centuries as the leading international financial centre. The importance of London is reflected in the fact that all but eight of the world's fifty largest banks as calculated by the *Banker* in mid-1975 had a stake in at least one and, in many cases several, London Euro-banks.[9]

While London has attracted the great majority of Euro-banks because of the size and efficiency of its interbank and other markets, a somewhat smaller number of these banks have set up operations in other money centres. While an active interbank dealing market usually exists in these centres and a certain amount of loan syndication takes place, London generally is a substantial net provider of funds to both the interbank and syndication markets in these other centres, particularly in periods of credit stringency. Excluding tax haven centres such as the Bahamas and the Grand Caymans where some Euro-banks may be legally incorporated with operating headquarters elsewhere, the sub-markets with a particularly large concentration of Euro-banks are Luxembourg, Singapore, and Hong Kong. In each case, the amount of locally-oriented business done by Euro-banks is nominal or non-existent, as the choice of location has been based on the factors of cost, proximity to growing market areas, tax, flexibility of regulation, ease of entry and communications.

Each of these and other centres offers different trade-offs to the stockholders of Euro-banks, and extensive feasibility studies generally precede the decision to open in one centre or another. For some of the largest American, British and European banks, some form of participation in each major Eurocurrency centre, often through a Euro-bank affiliate, is considered necessary, whereas smaller banks tend to concentrate their international overseas operations in a more limited number of locations.

The management issues faced by Euro-bankers in different financial centres must obviously be dealt with in the economic, and regulatory and market context of their particular financial centre. Tax structure, ratio and other regulatory requirements imposed by local authorities, operating cost structure, the extent of and access to local currency business, time zone and other factors relating to communications, availability of trained staff, exchange controls, local political and economic conditions and other factors all have a significant impact on the management of Euro-banks in these centres. As discussed in subsequent chapters, however, the key Euro-bank management issues which are the subject of this book are not primarily a function of location, so that the following paragraphs summarise only briefly the structure and factors which have led to the establishment of Euro-banks in centres outside the principal one of London.

Luxembourg, where a total of fifty-nine banks, including thirty-seven subsidiary banks and nine consortium institutions, had established themselves as of September, 1975, offers Euro-banks a relatively low operating cost structure and the same time zone for trading purposes as London. Most importantly, it has offered German banks a convenient locus for Eurocurrency business which avoids such Bundesbank regulations as reserve requirements on international business which otherwise would exclude them from participation in the market. Roughly twenty-five Luxembourg banks are thus owned individually or collectively by German banks.[10] In addition, a number of other Luxembourg-based Euro-banks are owned by Belgian, North American and other European financial institutions attracted by cost, convenience, tax, linguistic and other factors.

The principal Eurocurrency market in Asia is Singapore, which has sponsored the development since 1968 of the Asia-dollar market through a policy of selective entry into, and careful supervision of, the international money market there. Profiting from its central location in rapidly growing South Asia, its political stability as well as low tax and operating costs, the Singaporean government had granted licenses by mid-1975 to over sixty banks to deal in the Eurocurrency (or Asia-dollar) market through Asian Currency Units (ACUs) which had total assets at end-1974 of $10,000 million.[11] While most of this international deposit and lending activity is carried on by the branches of large international banks, in September 1974 there were nineteen 'merchant banks' generally owned by American, Japanese and European financial institutions, often with local partners, who have set up wholly-owned or consortium subsidiaries on a regional basis to carry on an international investment and commercial banking business with emphasis on medium-term Eurocurrency lending to Asian borrowers.[12]

The other major Asian centre for Euro-banks is Hong Kong, which offers much the same advantages as Singapore as well as a more relaxed regulatory climate. While a withholding tax on interest paid has restrained the development of a money market competitive with that of Singapore, this tax can easily be avoided by channeling Eurocurrency transactions outside the colony. As of July 1974, a total of forty-six foreign owned Euro-banks had been set up, mostly since 1972, by North American, Japanese and European financial institutions on a wholly-owned or consortium basis to specialise in Asian-oriented investment and commercial banking business.[13]

Attracted by the importance of the French economy and financial markets, a number of Euro-banks have also been established in Paris despite the general concern on the part of foreign bankers with regard to what is often considered excessive control of their activities by the Banque de France. Several of the older Euro-banks were opened in Paris, while more recent additions include Arab-oriented consortium banks with strong French sponsorship. In addition to these four markets, individual Euro-banks have been set up in recent years in Brussels, Beirut, Zurich, Geneva and other cities.

While a few Euro-banks have existed for several decades and grown with the Euromarkets, the great majority has been established since the mid-1960s. In most cases the founding stockholders have been commercial banks, although in some cases other institutions such as mutual funds, insurance companies, investment banks, brokerage houses and industrial corporations have helped found new Euro-banks. Numerically, most of the Euro-banks are consortium-owned by two or more stockholders; a large number are wholly-owned subsidiaries of financial institutions, and a few are widely held and quoted on a stock exchange.

The objectives and strategies of the Euro-bank vary widely. Most of the earlier consortium banks were established to enable their stockholders to participate in the medium-term Eurocurrency lending market to which they otherwise would not have access. More recent consortia have been set up to specialise in a specific geographic area such as Scandinavia, Latin America, the Pacific Basin or Eastern Europe or a specific functional sector such as energy or shipping project finance. In many cases, government ownership of Euro-banks gives them a semi-official role in the market. Wholly-owned or controlled subsidiaries have been established by many large American and other commercial banks to diversify into investment banking activities, while a variety of banks and non-banking groups have preferred to use a separately capitalised vehicle rather than a branch to extend their operations into the Eurocurrency and Eurobond markets. While no Euro-bank has been established without a well-articulated set of objectives, there is little doubt in many cases that the competitive desire to respond to the founding of a Euro-bank by a rival institution was the key motivation behind the setting up of a new Euro-bank. In the late 1960s, a stake in a new London-based bank became for many banks a fashionable portion of an expansion strategy.

In mid-1975, a list of specific objectives for the Euro-banks in the London market might include one or more of the following:

(1) enable a commercial bank (particularly Japanese or American owned, in the context of Edge Act legislation) to diversify into investment banking activities such as underwriting, securities dealing and the taking of equity interests.

(2) earn a higher return on capital than the parent can in its traditional activities;

(3) place surplus funds generated by stockholder banks into the international interbank market and enable stockholders to participate in Eurocurrency syndicated loans;

(4) enable banks with little international experience to become acquainted with the international deposit and lending market;

(5) serve in effect as an international branch in a specific financial centre for stockholder banks which are unable to establish one due to local or home country regulations;

(6) attract international funds to the country or region in which the stockholders are located or to the parent itself;

(7) serve as a common vehicle for a formal or informal grouping of individual banks with similar interests or objectives;

(8) represent the parent bank in a major international money market to expand its international network;

(9) extend the range of international services provided the parents' domestic customers, in particular if competitor banks already have a significant Euromarket base;

(10) serve as a marketing vehicle for the syndicated loans generated by the network of a large parent bank;

(11) serve as a focal point for a number of international banks interested in doing business in a particular country or region;

(12) enable a non-banking institution to participate in the Eurocurrency market; and

(13) enable stockholders to participate in the medium-term Eurocurrency lending market in general or in a specific type of lending such as shipping or energy finance.

The stockholder ties among consortium banks extend from purely *ad hoc* arrangements built around that consortium venture to a closely integrated group which co-operates in other sectors as well. In certain instances the Euro-bank acts as a direct extension of the parents' activities which may severely restrict the areas of activity open to the Euro-bank, whereas in others a more opportunistic approach is taken with the ultimate object to maximise profitability. A number of large international banks such as Barclays and Bank of America have participated in the formation of a variety of Euro-banks throughout the world, while others have expanded only through their branch networks or a limited number of specialised or wholly-owned subsidiaries.

A number of Euro-bank ownership patterns have evolved over the past decade. First, the wholly-owned subsidiary is usually established by a relatively large national bank to provide a particular service or fill a specific gap in the parent's geographic network which another corporate entity cannot. Such subsidiaries may act as the Euro-currency loan syndicating arm of a large US money centre bank, operate in financial markets where the parent cannot legally open a branch, perform an underwriting function which would be illegal in a different corporate form or simply provide a more flexible management environment than would be the case for a branch.

A second ownership pattern is that of the majority-controlled subsidiary with a limited number of minority partners. The corporate objectives of such a bank may be similar to that of the wholly-owned subsidiary — to conduct specialist activities or operate in a limited geographic market — but minority shareholders have been brought in to provide a local partner, specialist expertise or other requirements to achieve stated objectives. Local partners represent an obvious choice for a foreign bank entering a new market and may even represent a prerequisite for entry by local authorities, while other minority stockholders may provide a source of funds or new business contacts as well as market experience.

A broad ownership range with no single dominant stockholder represents the third ownership pattern. In some of these cases, a single bank — often a London merchant bank — has taken the initiative of bringing together into a single consortium a relatively large number of foreign banks who may be characterised by their lack of international financial expertise, interest in becoming involved in a particular geographic or functional sector of the Euro-currency market or common background — such as ownership by savings or co-operative banks. Many of the earlier consortium banks were established on the basis of historically strong personal or business ties among banks from a variety of countries who felt that a minority stake in a consortium bank was the best approach to the rapidly growing Eurocurrency market. A trend in the late 1960s towards the formation of international banking 'clubs' of banks committed to work together internationally without a legal merger, resulted in the formation of a number of consortia designed to embody this co-operative commitment.

Single country or regional consortia are composed of banks from a given country or region who come together to pool their resources in a venture they would not undertake individually because of limited financial or personnel resources; in the case of countries such as Japan, such a pooling of resources may be a prerequisite to receiving official approval to establish an overseas entity, while several Scandinavian groupings have been set up on the basis of historical ties among the Nordic countries. A different type of multi-bank regional consortium is one whose marketing objectives rather than ownership pattern relates to a particular country or region. Such banks bring together a variety of international banks often chosen to provide the widest possible geographic representation, and one or more banks from a specific country or region such as Eastern Europe, Latin America or the Arab countries to develop business specifically in that country or region.

A full range of possible Euro-bank activities would include the following:

(1) taking of call, short date and fixed date Eurocurrency deposits of up to several years from the interbank market and customers to fund the bank's own loan portfolio and for relending in the interbank market;

(2) exchange dealing in spot and forward Eurocurrencies and often the local currency of the stockholder for the account of clients, the bank's own position or to create deposits through the swap;

(3) Eurocurrency lending for the banks' own book on a rollover or fixed rate basis from short dates to medium-term (the latter having exceeded ten years at various times in recent years) to governments and government agencies, corporations and individuals throughout the world on a secured or unsecured basis. Often lending activity in the local currency of the market in which the bank is located represents a significant portion of the portfolio.

(4) management of Eurocurrency rollover loans on an underwriting or best efforts basis to be placed with the stockholder group or a wider range of banks;

(5) origination, management, underwriting and selling of publicly issued Eurobonds and Euroequities; provision of a secondary trading market in Eurobonds;

(6) arrangement of private placements of fixed-rate debt issues in a variety of currencies with international investors;

(7) corporate finance activities such as project structuring, corporate restructuring and mergers and acquisitions;

(8) provision of traditional trade finance or correspondent banking services through the opening of letters of credit, acceptance finance, money transfer and collection;

(9) portfolio management for international investors;

(10) arrangement of lease finance either with or without the use of a tax shield;

(11) arrangement of export finance through one or more national export credit agencies;

(12) the taking of equity participations either on an outright basis or in connection with the extension of a loan;

(13) specialist project financing capability in sectors such as energy and shipping.

Few Euro-banks are active in all these sectors, and many limit themselves for practical purposes to Eurocurrency lending and the deposit and exchange dealing necessary to support this activity. Certain banks, which are often described as merchant banks, emphasise fee generation through the origination and syndication of Euro-loans and Euro-bonds, whereas at the other extreme some banks derive earnings primarily through interest differential income on Eurocurrency loans taken from other banks. The latter banks usually possess a relatively large capital base compared with that of the investment banking or fee-oriented institutions. Net stockholder funds including subordinated debt for the sample of forty banks ranged from £1 million to £30 million at the end of fiscal 1974.

The management of most Euro-banks is usually characterised by a higher degree of autonomy than would exist in the home office or a direct branch of a parent shareholder. Justified by such factors as the different nature of the subsidiary's activity, time and geographic distance, and the express desire of the stockholders to create a more flexible and opportunistic vehicle than the parent, this relative autonomy can be significantly restricted in the event of poor operating results of the Euro-bank or the advent of a cautious lending or investing policy on the part of the parents. Senior management of a Euro-bank is usually either seconded from a stockholder bank or recruited from one of the major international commercial banks, an investment or merchant bank or another Euro-bank.

In many cases an experienced, mature chief executive is chosen from one of the British clearing banks or similar institutions on the basis of his relatively conservative approach to his responsibilities, whereas in other situations a relatively young man is attracted to the position on the basis of its relative autonomy and compensation, which may include an incentive element.

Given the dual investment and commercial banking objectives of many Euro-banks and the relatively small number of qualified individuals with experience in both sectors, locating appropriate senior management has not been an easy task for Euro-bank sponsors. In view of the importance of interest differential income, their familiarity with these activities and the relative ease of generating this type of income, many stockholder banks have engaged individuals with essentially commercial banking backgrounds after unsuccessful attempts to locate the ideal individual with experience in both commercial and investment banking.

Entry into the London market for a new Euro-bank has not been difficult for a bank with backing from established financial institutions. The British authorities have welcomed new entrants to an international market centre which they have deliberately freed from restrictions imposed by other national authorities, and the principal barrier to entry is authorisation by the Bank of England to deal in foreign exchange and foreign currency deposits. In recent years, such approval has been granted following a relatively brief trial period to the Euro-bank affiliates of foreign banking institutions of a size and stature the Bank considers adequate to provide sufficient support to the London affiliate. No minimum capital guidelines have been established, although in recent years most new Euro-banks have opened up with an initial paid-in capital of at least several million pounds. The Bank also vets the qualifications and reputation of senior management, in particular those of the senior money manager of the new bank.

The UK regulatory climate in which the London-based Euro-bank operates involves a minimum of specific guidelines and an emphasis on flexible, personal, evolving and participative supervision.[14] Euro-banks are regulated in the same fashion as local UK banks engaged primarily in the sterling market and are therefore subject to the same complex Exchange Control regulations. Eurocurrency business which does not involve UK residents or sterling transactions is effectively unregulated, and since the sterling business of most Euro-banks is a small fraction of their total activity, these banks achieve a freedom of operation which is fairly unique in a major money centre.

In contrast to the extensive ratio and credit controls applied to banks established in other major financial centers, the only numerical ratio guideline applied to banks established in the UK in mid-1975 is the minimum reserve ratio applied to sterling deposits for purposes of monetary policy control. As of mid-1975, this required that a minimum of 12½ per cent of sterling deposit liabilities not used to finance sterling interbank assets be held in such reserve assets as cash at the Bank of England, money at call in the London Discount Market and certain government securities. In the event, Euro-banks have generally maintained ratios significantly in excess of this minimum. Selective and general controls on sterling lending have been imposed from time to time in the past, but as of mid-1975 none were in effect.

The Euro-banks discussed in the following chapters are primarily UK-incorporated banks owned by foreign stockholders, although there have been included a few branches of foreign Euro-banks which derive a significant portion of their earnings from their London branch. Operating generally from a single office in the City of London, these banks usually are organised along functional lines with separate money market/Euro-bond, lending, credit, administrative and corporate finance departments reporting to a chief executive. The size of staff is a function of the bank's overall volume of business, the extent of personnel-intensive functions such as documentary credit or bond dealing operations, the relative importance of services to be provided stockholders or clients, and the extent of business development and loan syndication activities carried on by the Euro-bank. In late 1974 a survey by the *Banker* of separately capitalised operating Eurocurrency banks in London showed staff levels ranging from eleven to 160 with an average of fifty-seven.[15] For the thirty-five Euro-banks which indicated staff as well as asset levels at that time, the amount of assets per employee extended from a low of £.3 million to a high of £10.5 million with an average of £2.9 million. The highest asset/employee figures were shown by Euro-banks whose principal activity lies in taking participations in medium-term Eurocurrency loans and funding these loans, with the lowest ratios indicated by banks with major loan generation and syndication as well as Euro-bond activities.

London-based Euro-banks often have established overseas branches, affiliates and representative offices. Euro-bank officers may be posted to the parent bank's country as well as major overseas market areas such as the Pacific Basin, Latin America or the Arab Gulf for business development purposes. Participations are taken in Euro-banks, often affiliated with the stockholder groups, in other market centres; quite often the London-based Euro-bank acts as the co-ordinating vehicle for the worldwide investment banking network of a large international bank or informal 'club' of such banks. Investments are made by Euro-banks in London or overseas-based non-banking institutions such as financial service, leasing and venture capital companies to provide a broader range of customer services.

The chapters which follow provide a detailed analysis of Euro-bank asset management (Chapter 3), liability management (Chapter 4), other income-producing activities (Chapter 5), and an analysis of Euro-bank profitability (Chapter 6). The chapters are based in large part on my own personal experience and observations from eight years in the Euromarkets, but to provide a broader and more representative spectrum of experience a total of forty in-depth interviews have been held with the senior management, in most cases the chief executive, of Euro-banks whose principal base of activity and source of revenue is the London market.

The sample includes most of the London consortium banks in operation in mid-1975, a number of wholly-owned subsidiaries of American and European banks, and London branches of foreign Euro-banks who derive most of their income from the Eurocurrency markets. A similar sample could have been taken in other centres such as Luxembourg or Hong Kong which would bring out peculiarities of these particular markets. Given the absolute and relative importance of London as well as the significance both individually and collectively of the London Euro-banks, I believe that the following analysis will more than adequately deal with the critical issues facing Euro-banks in the mid 1970s.

One possible weakness of the sample interviews is that too much emphasis might be placed on current management policies in response to contemporary market conditions and problems, as opposed to strategies dealing with fundamental management issues. By emphasising the latter in our discussions, however, and placing these conversations in the context of a longer-term personal involvement in the Eurocurrency market, I hope I have effectively dealt with this issue. Appendix 1 lists the forty banks included in the statistical sample, which contains all but one of the banks interviewed.

APPENDIX I
BANKS INCLUDED IN STATISTICAL SAMPLE
(amounts in m.)

Bank	Date Established	Total Assets at End-1974[a]	Total Stockholder Funds at End-1974[a]
Banque Belge Limited	1934	£112.4	£8.4
Midland and International Banks Limited	1964	£654.4	£29.7
Dow Banking Corporation	1965	SF989.5	SF142.0
International Commercial Bank Limited	1967	£387.8	£19.7
Rothschild Intercontinental Bank Limited[c]	1967	£384.0	£21.8
Allied Bank International	1968	$593.5	$38.4
Brown Harriman & International Banks Limited	1968	£70.3	£4.6
Manufacturers Hanover Limited	1968	£48.4	£3.3
Western American Bank (Europe) Limited	1968	£133.3	£27.5
Atlantic International Bank	1969	£69.3	£6.0
Bankers Trust International Limited	1969[b]	£114.1	£7.3
Scandinavian Bank Limited	1969	£344.0	£18.2
Associated Japanese Bank (International) Limited	1970	£295.9	£18.8
Japan International Bank Limited	1970	£248.2	£16.0
London Multinational Bank Limited	1970	£258.3	£13.2
Orion Bank Limited	1970	£550.0	£23.7
United International Bank Limited	1970	£163.5	£8.5
Bank of America International Limited	1971	£238.3	£12.0
Edward Bates & Sons (Holdings) Limited	1971[b]	£68.3	£7.6
International Marine Banking Co. Limited	1971	£264.0	£12.8
London Interstate Bank Limited	1971	£45.9	£6.1
Nordic Bank Limited	1971	£209.2	£13.6
Credit Suisse White Weld Limited	1971[b]	£30.3	£2.3
Continental Illinois Limited	1972	£125.3	£8.1
European Brazilian Bank Limited	1972	£133.3	£5.9
Italian International Bank Limited	1972	£147.4	£10.4
Libra Bank Limited	1972	£142.6	£7.6
Merrill Lynch—Brown Shipley Bank Limited	1972	£42.3	£4.0
UBAF Limited	1972	£208.3	£10.8
Wells Fargo Limited	1972	£108.5	£6.1
Anglo-Romanian Bank Limited	1973	£35.2	£1.6
Banco Urquijo Limited	1973	£27.4	£2.3
European Banking Company Limited	1973	£171.4	£10.5
First International Bancshares Limited	1973	£67.3	£8.2
Hungarian International Bank Limited	1973	£34.4	£3.0
International Energy Bank Limited	1973	£41.1	£10.2
Iran Overseas Investment Bank Limited	1973	£27.3	£5.0
London and Continental Bankers Limited	1973	£152.2	£11.1
Banque de Bruxelles Drayton Limited	1974	£12.8	£1.0
International Mexican Bank Limited	1974	£19.6	£2.5

[a]Year-end approximately 31 Dec 74. For banks with fiscal years ending up to and including 30 June, latest figures available at the time of writing have been used.
[b]Banks originally established at earlier dates but began significant Eurocurrency operations in year indicated.
[c]Merged in 1975 with Amex Bank Ltd.

3 Asset Management

Asset management is one of the Euro-bank chief executive's highest priorities in view of the importance usually placed by stockholders on participation in the medium-term Eurocurrency deposit and lending market and the relative facility with which a loan portfolio can be built up to earn a return on invested capital. While many Euro-banks — particularly subsidiaries of the large American commercial banks — as a matter of policy do not carry a significant loan portfolio on their own books, interest differential income and fees derived from loan participations represent the dominant source of income for most Euro-banks.

While no officially published data covers the exact market segment represented by my definition of Euro-bank, Bank of England statistics on 'consortium banks', which represent the bulk of London Euro-bank assets, provide a useful indication of the asset breakdown for the typical Euro-bank. These data have only been published on this basis since mid-1975, but Table D provides a detailed breakdown of consortium bank assets as of 16 July 1975.

TABLE D

ASSET COMPOSITION OF LONDON CONSORTIUM BANKS AS OF 16 JULY 1975
(amounts in £ m.)

Asset	Sterling	Foreign Currency	Total	
			Amount	% of Total
Reserve Assets	43	—	43	.8
Special Deposits	8	—	8	.1
Deposits with UK Banks + Discount Market	295	794	1089	19.9
Certificates of Deposit	67	202	269	4.9
Loans to UK Borrowers	306	359	665	12.1
Other Loans and Bills	32	3266	3298	60.1
Investments	36	33	69	1.3
Other Assets (including acceptances, etc.)[a]	44		44	.8
TOTAL	831	4654	5485	100.0

[a]Includes some non-sterling assets.
Source: *Bank of England Quarterly Bulletin*, vol. 15, no. 3 (Sep. 1975)
Tables 8/10 (new series).

Almost three-quarters of consortium bank assets in mid-1975 were represented by customer loans, principally to overseas borrowers in Eurocurrencies, with the bulk of the remainder applied to interbank deposits and certificates of deposit. Sterling assets as of July 1975 accounted for only 15 per cent of total assets. With the exception of several wholly-owned Euro-bank subsidiaries of US banks, the asset composition of non-consortium London Euro-banks should not differ significantly from the figures in Table D. Among the smaller asset categories, reserve assets accounted for less than 1 per cent of total assets; as of July 1975, the consortium bank reserve asset ratio was 21 per cent, significantly in excess of the 12½ per cent minimum requirement. Investments of 1.3 per cent of assets represent primarily holdings of UK government securities and Euro-bonds.

For day-to-day liquidity purposes, Euro-banks rely on prime bank certificates of deposits as well as money at call in the discount market, short-term loans to other banks and possibly a short date gilt portfolio. While during the early 1970s a wide variety of London banks issued dollar and sterling certificates of deposit, during the 1974 crisis of confidence following the Franklin and Herstatt failures, the market for all but the most prime names – generally the top ten US banks and British clearing banks – dried up to the extent that banks looking for liquidity in their certificate of deposit portfolio felt obliged to concentrate on these prime names.

The two principal asset categories are loans to other banks and customer loans. The ratio between these two, which is one of the few which is usually revealed in published data and considered relevant by the management of some Euro-banks, is a matter of debate both as to its significance as well as to the appropriate ratio. Loans to other banks, which are made for periods of up to one year and in some cases longer, generally provide a minimal return to the lending bank if matched by a corresponding deposit. The ⅛ per cent spread between the quoted bid and asked rates in the London interbank market provides a theoretical indication of the interest margin available on such loans. In practice, particularly during periods of market nervousness, Euro-banks are rarely among those institutions able to take funds at the bid rate, and since the tiering of the interbank market in the form of offered rates quoted as a function of a borrower's presumed creditworthiness has become more prevalent following the 1974 crisis, they often find themselves paying the offered rate or even higher.

While it is therefore possible to make a marginal spread on an interbank loan by lending on a matched basis to another bank which pays more for its money than the lending institution, the presumed credit risk involved limits the extent of this business. In practice, interbank lending on a matched basis for many Euro-banks involves a breakeven or even marginal loss operation, particularly if their lending is concentrated on the prime names in the market such as the major US, UK and Continental banks.

In view of this profit constraint, the extent of most Euro-banks' lending to other banks is a function of the desired level of liquidity, published balance sheet ratios, the need to maximise profits and the importance of being seen by other banks to be both a lender as well as a taker of interbank funds. While fixed-term loans to other banks presumably involve a minimal level of risk, breaking such a deposit for liquidity purposes would be considered one of the last ditches of defense in a crisis. As for the appropriate ratio for balance sheet purposes, most Euro-bankers agree that there is no ideal relationship between interbank loans and other assets in view of the great differences among banks in terms of leverage, quality of assets and business objectives. Those bankers that have a specific relationship in mind usually think in terms of a fifty-fifty ratio between interbank and customer loans, with a few others aiming at a smaller portion of interbank loans.

As a result, the principal objective of Euro-banks in maintaining a given amount of interbank loans is to be seen to be operating on both sides of the interbank market. While it is universally recognised that Euro-banks are generally net takers of interbank funds, a bank feels that being able to make a two-way quote to other banks reflects favourably both on its credit rating and its professionalism. In times of market stress and nervousness, making such a two-way market for practical purposes may involve lending out short date (up to one week in maturity) rather than fixed date (from one week to one year) funds both because of liquidity objectives and the relative unavailability of longer date deposits.

The management of the customer loan portfolio is often regarded by the chief executive as his principal priority. The implicit priority tradition-ally given by bankers to loan quality is reinforced among Euro-bankers by their institutions' newness to the market and corresponding relative lack of substantial retained earnings to meet potential losses. The normal sense of professionalism in terms of one's loss record is thus heightened by the practical knowledge that one's profitability if not viability as well as the path of one's career are vitally dependent on minimising loan losses. On the other hand, the easy availability of loan participations through the syndication process and the historically almost unique phenomenon of starting a new business with a large capital base but no loans, created strong pressures to build up a large loan portfolio in a short period of time. Throughout history new banks have usually built up their base of stockholder funds through retained earnings from the gradual and profit-able build-up of assets and new capital which is attracted by this profitable growth. On the contrary, the typical Euro-banker on opening for business often finds himself with a paid-in capital of at least several million pounds, a substantial overhead to amortise and the implicit or spoken requirement to meet certain earnings targets which in reality can only be met in the short term by putting loans on the books. To these powerful incentives is added the natural human desire of the chief executive to produce an earnings record and build a significant asset base.

Torn by these conflicting pressures, the Euro-banker responds by building a loan portfolio which in his mind best balances the objectives of minimal individual credit risk, diversification of risk, attractive profitability, shortest maturity and any other specific objectives established by the stockholders. The latter may relate to geographic or industry specialisation, maturity, the relative importance of own-generated business and other factors.

Individual credit risk, the evaluation of which is usually viewed by the banker as his professional stock in trade, also poses some of the most difficult problems in view of the nature of today's Eurocurrency market. Historically, loss experience in international lending has been extremely low; a 1972 study by the Federal Reserve staff of overseas lending by US banks found it to have been a fraction of domestic loan loss experience.[1] It can be argued, however, that this excellent experience was a function of an unchecked boom in world trade and investment; that most international business was done in the 1950s and 1960s with prime multinational companies who have rarely failed to meet their own and their subsidiaries' obligations, and that the business was being carried on primarily by large American and European commercial banks with significant international lending experience.

On the other hand, Euro-banks are much more dependent on business taken from the syndication market, which at least implies that the very best business from a credit standpoint may be held in portfolio by the syndicating banks rather than sold to the market. It is quite apparent, for example, that short term finance for their corporate customers, which traditionally has been the backbone of international banking, is generally kept within the portfolio of major international banks, and Euro-banks usually participate in the business only if it is channeled to them by a parent bank. More importantly, the nature of Eurocurrency lending has shifted markedly during the 1970s towards longer maturities, a greater involvement in finance for large projects with a significant commodity, technological or competitive risk; and a much larger component of country risk, in particular countries which do not have a long or positive record of borrowing from the private banking sector. In 1974, for example, borrowers from a total of sixty-two different countries were shown in publicised credits listed by the International Bank for Reconstruction and Development.

Faced with these constraints and the obvious difficulty in evaluating so many of the credits available to him, the Euro-banker may respond in several ways to the challenge of risk control. One alternative is to opt for 'name' credits which are generally accepted in the marketplace and/or by the stockholders as involving at worst only a nominal risk and not necessitating any original credit work. While what constitutes an acceptable 'name' may change over time, major Western governments and their agencies and prime multinational corporations generally fall into this category. In such cases, the principal decision variables are pricing, amount, maturity and possibly reciprocity. The implicit assumption in accepting such risks is often the apocalyptic argument to the effect that 'if X borrower defaults, then none of us will be around anyway to worry about collecting our principal.'

Another option is to rely on the parent bank or banks' credit judgement, which not only brings to bear the worldwide resources and credit information capabilities of a major international bank but also serves to shift responsiblity from the Euro-bank executive to his stockholder in the event of future problems. Euro-bankers often admit to ignorance of a specific country but are prepared to participate in a credit because a stockholder is 'happy with the risk'. In a typical Euro-bank's control procedure, the extremely difficult question of country risk exposure is a matter of periodic dialogue with Board members who presumably bring to bear the particular expertise of their own institutions to set and revise country limits with the result that level of country risk is usually a shared decision. In many cases, the Euro-bank's country exposure is computed within the parent bank or banks' overall exposure to a given country or classification of countries, and a continual dialogue between management and stockholders revolves around the former's share of this global quota.

A third response is that of making independent judgements on the basis of the Euro-banks' own credit expertise. While most if not all Euro-banks have a separate credit department, in many instances this function is primarily an administrative one concerned with the mechanical spreading of statements, analysis of data and monitoring of existing loans, rather than an independent source of lending judgement. In making most credit decisions, reliance is usually placed by the chief executive on his own credit judgement or that of a few very experienced colleagues. In many cases Euro-banks have developed specialised expertise in industrial sectors such as shipping, real estate or energy financing or in certain geographic areas which is the province of key individuals in the bank's management or that of its stockholders; other banks often rely heavily on this specialist knowledge in taking participations in loans to sectors in which they have no direct experience. To the extent which their human resources and decision-making autonomy permit, individual Euro-banks form an independent judgement on individual country, sectoral and corporate risks through extensive travel, independent financial analysis of corporate borrowers and maintenance of contacts with a given industry.

Diversification of risk is one of the few variables in the management of the loan portfolio which can be controlled directly by the chief executive. Depending on the individual management's philosophy, a variety of control systems may be employed. Most banks have a maximum limit on exposure to one borrower or a related group of borrowers which generally ranges between 10—20 per cent of stockholders' funds. For banks with a relatively low absolute capital, the percentage may be a bit higher to enable them to take a $1 million participation in a given syndication. For banks which recognise a maximum exposure limit, there is often a distinction made by maturity (i.e. a higher percentage of net worth for short term loans) and by country (i.e. — a highly favoured government merits a higher percentage exposure).

On the other hand, a number of banks maintain a large degree of flexibility in this respect. One category of these banks is comprised of Euro-banks with a specific vocation which emphasises the attracting of funds to a specific country or group of countries such as the Socialist bloc or Latin America. Placing a limit on exposure to the sole borrower in a Socialist country which sponsors that particular Euro-bank is naturally regarded as self-defeating. Another category is comprised of wholly-owned and consortium banks who regard themselves as an extension of their stockholders and therefore able to rely on the latters' resources. For a borrower who is a highly valued customer of one of the stockholders, several Euro-banks are prepared to lend up to and beyond their capital base with implicit support both as to credit and possible balance sheet assistance from a parent.

Country risk control represents another variable in the diversification of risk. Virtually all Euro-banks recognise that any absolute limit established is a highly judgemental and subjective decision, although a number of banks or their parents perform laborious analytical exercises by which individual countries' economic statistics are examined and different factors determining a country's ability and willingness to provide foreign exchange to meet its debts are analysed and weighted. Among the factors given significant consideration is a forward analysis of debt servicing capability as measured by dividing foreign currency debt service by projected exports and invisible income. Most bankers recognise that even this calculation must be refined significantly by judgemental factors; witness the fact that in mid-1975 these ratios for such relatively popular borrowers as Mexico and Brazil were a significant multiple of those for Portugal and other less popular countries, while similar data for the highly regarded Socialist countries are simply not available.

To the extent that any formula approach is applied to country risk, a limitation based on the Euro-bank's capital or percentage of loans outstanding seems to be most prevalent. Such a percentage, which might be 10 per cent of one's total portfolio or 50—100 per cent of one's net worth, is usually applied to less developed or other countries outside those represented by the stockholders groups, in which countries presumably such risks are acceptable or actually desirable from a strategic standpoint.

In practice, given the regional preferences of banks set up to specialise in Latin America, the Arab world, Asia or the Socialist bloc, Euro-banks sponsored in such a fashion often have a preponderant proportion of their portfolio so allocated, and the risk of loss arising from such lack of geographic diversification is regarded by the chief executive as relating to the strength of the stockholder banks rather than his own balance sheet. While country risk control is thus given an apparent high priority by management, its limitations for the reasons given above are usually frankly admitted by management. One consortium bank executive who has a highly refined country risk control system pointed out that his only potential loan losses to date were located in the US and UK, the only countries for which limits had not been established because of the presumed absence of country risk. Bankers also admitted to the flexibility of country limits in the event of a change in economic or political climate, the appearance of an interesting piece of business or another opportunistic factor. Bankers also recognise that modifying a country limit upon receipt of unfavourable news does not eliminate an existing exposure which may still have several years to run, while there is some intellectual inconsistency in changing basic lending policy in response to short term developments such as the decision by stockholder banks' official examiners to classify a given type of risk, unexpected political events and episodic occurrences such as the discovery of oil.

Other limits placed for purposes of diversification of risk usually relate to exposure to industries or sectors which are perceived to carry a certain risk in aggregate. These limitations have been placed in recent years on sectors borrowing heavily from the Eurocurrency market such as shipping, real estate and the petroleum industry which often happen to be the specialist preserve of a number of Euro-banks. In practice, however, these limits have a discontinuous or *ex post* characteristic in the sense that no further exposure to such a sector is permitted if internal analysis or market sentiment results in a negative management attitude toward the sector.

Very little official data on the composition of Euro-bank loan portfolios has been published, and individual banks have been reluctant to divulge even the broader industrial or geographic categories making up their portfolios. Of some assistance in evaluating such portfolios in general, however, is Bank of England data on the total non-sterling assets (claims) by borrowing country of all UK banks. Euro-banks represent only a small portion of this total, and their typical loan portfolio probably differs somewhat from the sectoral total because of the relatively high proportion of non-corporate customer related, syndicated loan business in portfolio as well as other factors, but Table E, which provides sectoral data as of end-1974, should give some indication of the extent of geographic diversification.

If one groups exposure to banks together with non-banks to obtain overall country exposure, UK banks have the largest exposure to Japan (13.4 per cent), the US (9.9 per cent), the Bahamas and various Western European members of the BIS. The relative importance of Belgium/Luxembourg, Bahamas, Panama, Singapore and Hong Kong is a reflection of the importance of these sub-Euromarkets as takers of Eurocurrency

TABLE E

NON-STERLING EXTERNAL CLAIMS OF UK BANKS BY BORROWING COUNTRY
AS OF 31 DECEMBER 1974
(amount in £ m.)

Country	Total Amount	% of Total UK Claims	of which: Loans to Banks Amount	of which: Loans to Banks % of Total	of which: Loans to other Borrowers Amount	of which: Loans to other Borrowers % of Total
Japan	5872	13.4	5566	18.0	306	2.4
US	4354	9.9	3136	10.1	1218	9.4
Italy	3205	7.3	2096	6.8	1109	8.6
Bahamas	3025	6.9	2968	9.6	57	.4
Belgium	2571	5.9	2327	7.5	244	1.9
France	2217	5.1	2069	6.7	148	1.1
West Germany	2115	4.8	1596	5.2	519	4.0
Switzerland	1441	3.3	1098	3.6	343	2.6
Brazil	1270	2.9	316	1.0	954	7.4
Singapore	1238	2.8	1218	3.9	20	.2
Netherlands	1187	2.7	882	2.9	305	2.4
Panama	1085	2.5	557	1.8	528	4.1
Hong Kong	965	2.2	726	2.3	239	1.8
Mexico	774	1.8	169	.6	605	4.7
Canada	712	1.6	602	2.0	110	.9
Norway	637	1.5	54	.2	619	4.8
Denmark	637	1.5	90	.3	547	4.2
Liberia	566	1.3	5	—	561	4.3
South Africa	566	1.3	22	.1	544	4.2
Greece	541	1.2	247	.8	294	2.3
USSR	521	1.2	511	1.7	10	.1
Spain	516	1.2	302	1.0	214	1.7
Finland	512	1.2	153	.5	359	2.8
TOTAL ALL COUNTRIES	43,880		30,919		12,961	

Source: Bank of England *Quarterly Bulletin*, vol. 15, no. 3 (Sep. 1975).

deposits from London banks. The largest non-bank borrowers are the US
(9.4 per cent), Italy (8.6 per cent), Brazil (7.4 per cent), Norway, Mexico
and Liberia. Perhaps the most significant conclusion to be drawn from
Table E is the wide extent of portfolio geographic diversification. While
Euro-banks have often been criticised for heavy lending to countries with
an above-average level of political and economic risk, in percentage terms
such exposure is quite diversified for the UK banking industy as a whole,
and the typical Euro-bank portfolio should not differ markedly from the
pattern indicated in Table E.

Another

/A third variable used to control a Euro-bank portfolio is maturity as measured either by average life or ultimate maturity. Average life is computed by dividing the total principal amount of a loan into the sum of each principal repayment multiplied by the period of time it is outstanding. /

Maturity is relevant both in terms of credit exposure and profitability in view of the market practice of fixing the interest spread throughout the life of a loan regardless of intervening changes in credit rating or market conditions. The relevance of variations in maturity is pointed up by Table F, which traces the pattern of final maturity period for regular borrowers on the Eurocurrency markets since 1972. *— 75   THBLE F*

While final maturity is only a rough measure of credit exposure or the period during which the lender is committed to a given level of return on funds invested, Table F shows how radical variations in this key indicator can be over a limited period of time. Over a three year period, for example, ISCOR final maturities ranged from eleven and one-half to three years, the Government of Brazil from fifteen to five years, the

TABLE F

FINAL MATURITY OF LOANS TO SELECTED MAJOR EUROCURRENCY
BORROWERS, JANUARY 1972 – JULY 1975

Borrower (Guarantor)		Date of Offering	Final Maturity (years)
South African Iron & Steel Corporation (ISCOR)	1973	Sep	11½
		Sep	10
		Dec	10
	1974	Apr	10
		Nov	5
	1975	Feb	3
		Mar	5
Government of Brazil	1972	Dec	12
	1973	Mar	10
		Apr	10
		Sep	10
		Sep	10
		Sep	10
		Nov	15
	1974	Feb	12
		June	12
		Dec	8
	1975	Jan	5
		Mar	10
		Apr	8
		May	5
		June	5

TABLE F (*Continued*)

Borrower (Guarantor)		Date of Offering	Final Maturity (years)
Republic of Peru	1972	Oct	7
		Dec	7
	1973	Apr	8
		Apr	7
		Sep	15
		Dec	10
	1974	Feb	10
		June	10
		July	10
		Dec	7
	1975	Mar	8
Banco Nacional de Obras y	1972	Jan	5
Servicios Publicos SA (Mexico)	1973	July	12
	1974	June	10
		July	8
		Oct	8
	1975	Mar	5
Imperial Government of Iran	1972	Apr	6
		June	7
		Nov	8
		Nov	8
		Nov	7
	1973	Feb	8
		Mar	8
		Aug	10
		Oct	10
		Oct	10
Bank of Greece	1972	Mar	10
		June	10
	1973	July	12
	1974	Mar	10
		Sep	8
Bank Handlowy W. Warszawie SA	1973	Apr	7
(Poland) (direct and as guarantor)		May	10
		June	10
		June	7
		Oct	10
		Nov	7
	1974	Feb	8
		Mar	8
		Apr	7
		July	7
		Sep	7
	1975	May	7
		June	5

Source: *Borrowing in International Capital Markets*, World Bank Document
E.C–181/752.

Republic of Peru from fifteen to seven years, Obras Publicos from twelve to five years and Bank Handlowy from ten to five years. Such fluctuations, which are as much a function of competition among banks as perceived credit risk, point up the key importance of timing in building a Eurocurrency portfolio.

Very few Euro-banks have established a permanent or semi-permanent maturity target, as expressed either in average life or ultimate maturity, which is built into the long term strategy of the bank. The great majority recognise their dependence on market conditions and inability to influence terms which in large part are established by larger banks in the market or 'competitive conditions'. Some chief executives go so far as to assume a passive role and to view their function as building a loan portfolio which reflects market conditions over an extended period of time. Others establish periodic guidelines which reflect both market conditions and the need to generate a certain minimum return on invested funds. During periods of vigorous competition for business such as existed in 1973 and early 1974, such a guideline may have implied a virtual absence from the market, whereas in early 1975, with a more favourable risk/reward pattern for the lender, this type of guideline may have enabled the lender to shorten his average life considerably with a significant degree of selectivity.

A number of banks have established maximum permissable final maturities and average lives at levels of, respectively, ten years and five years or higher, but during less competitive periods such as early 1975 they are able to set provisional maxima well within these limits. Throughout the first half of 1975, for example, Euro-banks have expressed almost unanimous agreement that an ultimate maturity of five years or possibly seven for selected project credits was the maximum acceptable, although many recognised that they might have to follow the market upward if the degree of competition increased. A few banks have established fairly permanent guidelines within the overall maturity pattern; several insist on keeping a proportion — say one-third or one-half — of customer loans under one year in final maturity to provide an appropriate maturity balance and insure a certain loan run-off should spreads increase.

The actual level of average life in the summer of 1975 for Euro-banks appears to range between two and four years with a heavy concentration around three years. In addition to the nature of the particular bank's asset portfolio, the timing of adding new loans on the books as indicated above is a highly relevant factor in determining this average.

The profitability of an individual loan or the portfolio as a whole is the final critical variable generally used to manage a Euro-bank loan portfolio. As in the case of maturity variability, loan spreads for comparable borrowers have fluctuated significantly during the past few years in response to a variety of factors which include credit as well as competitive considerations. Another component of loan profitability is represented by front end fees, which are particularly significant during lenders' markets and for credits which are relatively difficult to sell. Table G shows how,

TABLE G

INITIAL YEARS' INTEREST SPREAD (OVER LIBOR) FOR SELECTED MAJOR
EUROCURRENCY BORROWERS, JANUARY 1972–JULY 1975

Borrower		Date of Offering	Spread for Initial Years (%)
South African Iron and Steel	1973	Sep	$7/8$
Corporation (ISCOR)		Dec	$3/4$
	1974	Nov	$1^1/4$
	1975	Feb	$1^1/2$
		Mar	$1^3/4$
Government of Brazil (direct or as	1972	Dec	1
guarantor)	1973	Mar	1
		Apr	1
		Sep	1
		Sep	1
		Sep	1
		Nov	$5/8$
	1974	Feb	$5/8$
		June	$3/4$
		Dec	$1^1/2$
	1975	Jan	$1^3/4$
		Apr	$1^3/4$
		May	$1^3/4$
		June	$1^3/4$
Republic of Peru	1973	Apr	2
		Apr	$1^3/4$
		Dec	$1^1/4$
	1974	Feb	1
		June	$1^1/4$
		July	1
		Dec	$1^3/8$
	1975	Mar	$1^1/4$
Banco Nacional de Obras y Servicios	1973	July	$1/2$
Publicos SA (Mexico)	1974	June	$3/4$
		July	1
		Oct	$1^1/4$
	1975	Mar	$1^1/2$
Imperial Government of Iran	1972	Apr	$1^1/8$
		June	1
		Nov	$7/8$
		Nov	$7/8$
	1973	Feb	$3/4$
		Mar	$3/4$
		Aug	$5/8$
		Oct	$5/8$
		Oct	$5/8$

TABLE G (*Continued*)

Borrower		Date of Offering	Spread for Initial Years (%)
Bank of Greece	1972	Mar	1
		June	1
	1973	July	$^3/_4$
	1974	Mar	$^3/_4$
		Sep	$^3/_4$
Bank Handlowy W. Warszawie SA	1973	Apr	$^5/_8$
(Poland) (direct and as guarantor)		June	$^1/_2$
		June	$^1/_2$
		Oct	$^1/_2$
	1974	Feb	$^1/_2$
		Mar	$^7/_8$
		Apr	$^5/_8$
		July	$^5/_8$
		Sep	1
	1975	May	$1^1/_2$
		June	$1^1/_2$

Source: *Borrowing in International Capital Markets.* World Bank Group,
E.C–181/752.

for the same borrowers as in the previous maturity analysis, interest margins over LIBOR have moved for publicised credits since 1972 for the initial years of the outstanding loan.

During this three year period, spreads for initial maturities have fluctuated between ¾ per cent and 1¾ per cent for ISCOR, 5/8 per cent to 1¾ per cent for the Government of Brazil, 1¼ per cent to 2 per cent for the Government of Peru, ½ per cent to 1½ per cent for Obras Publicos, 5/8 per cent of 1⅛ per cent for the Government of Iran, and ½ per cent to 1½ per cent for Bank Handlowy. Unfortunately, sufficient data are not available on front end fees or other relevant variables which comprise overall return to the lender, but as these factors tend to move in line with interest margins, analysis of the latter should give a useful indication of the substantial variations of lending profitability over time. One of the unresolved issues in international lending is thus posed by the fact that, while pricing loans at a fixed margin over the cost of funds provides a theoretically assured gross margin, the practice of fixing a loan spread for a period of time which may exceed ten years substantially reduces the benefit of this innovation in loan pricing by preventing in most cases adjustments for changes in such critical variables as individual credit risk, rising operating costs or market conditions.

Within the constraints thus posed by the Eurocurrency pricing formula and competitive conditions, many Euro-banks have responded by establishing fairly permanent minimum lending spreads (including front end fees amortised over the life of the loan) for medium-term loans so as to provide a minimum return on invested funds given certain assumptions of maximum gearing, operating costs, etc. The figure most often mentioned in this context is 1 per cent over LIBOR. A more flexible view is taken on short-term credits of up to one year, which can be regarded as providing incremental earnings until full gearing is achieved. In addition, special exceptions may be made for clients particularly close to the bank or its parents, and allowance is usually made for other income which may be derived from the same customer to offset an otherwise unacceptable loan spread. On top of this permanent minimum spread, such banks establish more temporary higher guidelines in the context of individual planning periods and current market conditions; in mid-1975, for example, a margin of 1¼ per cent − 1½ per cent was regarded as the minimum acceptable for a prime credit on a medium-term basis. Some banks, on the other hand, feel that setting a target loan spread invites the taking of marginal credit risks, and a few of these banks refuse to consider loans with a spread exceeding a certain level on the assumption that a borrower paying more than a given interest margin is presumably not creditworthy.

A large number of Euro-banks, however, believe that establishing permanent guidelines which may force the bank out of the market for a period of time is not appropriate. In the view that they are a product of the market place, they believe that their performance can only be evaluated relatively in the context of that of similar banks rather than against an absolute standard of performance. Also, some managements feel that over an extended period of time the cycle of high and low spreads will average out to provide a reasonable return on invested funds without individual banks having to guess the timing of these moves. While such banks are prepared to establish provisional guidelines reflecting current market conditions, they take a much more flexible approach to the question of long-term loan profitability and often view the establishing of minimum acceptable spreads as wishful thinking.

The concept and adequacy of loan loss reserves is intimately related to management's policy with regard to loan profitability. While few Euro-banks are prepared to acknowledge that they are assuming anything but a first class credit risk in making a loan, the nature of much of the country and project lending of the mid-1970s, in addition to the actual or likely losses apparent on certain real estate and shipping loans in mid-1975, have obliged many banks to look more closely at the adequacy of their available reserves to support a significant loss.

When asked if they had in mind from a long-term, management planning standpoint a target loan loss reserve expressed presumably as a percentage of outstanding risk assets, somewhat over half of the Euro-bank executives felt that the concept was not relevant to their bank. These banks all acknowledged the necessity of reserving for specific realised or likely losses but felt that reserving additional, presumably taxed, amounts for management planning purposes was not valid. Many executives pointed out that all earnings would be retained in the bank for the foreseeable future to meet potential losses, and that, if these reserves were inadequate, the stockholders were capable of doing the necessary to restore the bank's viability. Several pointed to the excellent historical loss record in international lending and the difficulty of evaluating the ultimate loss potential inherent in possible country loan defaults.

The minority which felt that a general loss reserve above and beyond specific experience was a valid concept suggested percentage reserves which varied widely from ¾ per cent, which reflected domestic US experience, to 5 per cent, which presumed significant country loan losses. Most suggestions fell somewhat above or below 1½ per cent of outstanding customer loans. Many of these banks voiced a general concern that newer banks without substantial retained earnings might well find it difficult to accumulate a sufficient cushion of such earnings in the event of an unexpected disaster early in their corporate lives.

In their efforts to develop their loan portfolios, Euro-banks rely to a widely varying extent on business provided by stockholders, loans generated by the Euro-bank's own management team, and business introduced from the market in the form of loan syndications. In many cases, it was pointed out that the distinction between the first two is tenuous at best in view of the close working relationship with the stockholders in dealing with joint customers. Slightly over half of the forty banks in the sample felt that business generated by their own efforts plus those of the stockholders accounted for at least one-half of the loans currently in their portfolios, whereas a few banks were totally or almost completely reliant on business brought them from other banks. Some Euro-banks have extensive new business development efforts based on overseas representative offices and calling programs from London-based officers with geographic or functional responsiblities. Contributions of new business from parent banks of both wholly-owned and consortium Euro-banks varied from almost nothing to the bulk of the existing portfolio. The proportion of own-generated business seems to be more a function of the capabilities and preferences of the individual managements than any other factor.

In taking business from the market, most banks indicated that reciprocity was a significant factor assuming the credit and terms were reasonably acceptable; in a few cases the Euro-banks acknowledged that reciprocity was the principal reason for taking business from the market. Reciprocity in this context was measured by such factors as mutual interbank dealing relationships and willingness of the other bank to take loan syndications from the first bank.

In approving loan proposals, a variety of decision making procedures are utilised. At one extreme are the autonomous wholly-owned and consortium banks whose managements make all individual credit decisions without prior reference to non-executive members of the board of directors. At the other extreme are complex procedures of up to three or four ascending stages involving middle management, the chief executive, an executive committee of the board and the full board itself. In the case of wholly-owned subsidiaries, if reference to home office is necessary, a simple one—on—one contact between the chief executive and his organisational superior is usually sufficient. With consortium-owned banks, one or more stockholder representatives on the board are brought into the decision making process by the chief executive depending on the significance of the decision. For this purpose, the initial contact is often made by the chief executive with a committee based in London representing one or more of the stockholders which makes decisions on a quorum basis; for more significant decisions, a wider range of stockholder representatives may be contacted by telephone or telex; if one stockholder plays a dominant role in the consortium, a committee approach is often discarded.

The principal criterion determining reference to a higher authority than the chief executive is size of commitment. Many banks, however, also differentiate loan referrals on the basis of loan maturity, relationship to country limit and the presence of collateral security. Under these guidelines a chief executive will have greater autonomy, for example, if a given loan has a maturity of less than one year or if it is well within his country limit. Several chief executives emphasised the informal nature of the referral process to board members; particularly when a country risk or a customer known to a stockholder was involved, the chief executive preferred to share the decision with his executive committee even if the amount were well within his delegated limits.

The threshold amount beyond which the chief executives must refer a credit varies widely. In some cases the normal lending limit — say, 10—20 per cent of capital funds — can be committed by the chief executive, whereas in many consortium banks virtually all commitments of $1 million or more must be referred to a committee of the board.

A final lending policy issue is the relative importance of fixed rate as opposed to floating-rate lending. For analytical purposes, I have defined fixed-rate lending as any asset, either loan or quoted security, which has a maturity significantly in excess of a deposit of matching maturity and is not held for trading purposes. When there is a customer demand for fixed-rate loans of up to five years and more and deposits can be obtained for equivalent maturities, Euro-banks have often engaged in this type of lending. On other occasions, Euro-banks have been prepared to take a view on rates by extending a medium-term loan at a fixed rate without taking a matching deposit; in addition, some Euro-banks have acquired fairly significant sterling long date gilt edge portfolios for investment as opposed to trading purposes. In several cases such action was justified on the assumption that a portion of the bank's capital was being invested in quality, high yielding long-term assets. In practice, many of these quoted investments and offerings of fixed-rate loans were made in 1972—3 prior to the sharp world-wide upturn in interest rates in 1974, and enthusiasm for fixed-rate lending on an unmatched basis had diminished by mid-1975 to the extent that very few of the banks interviewed indicated any interest in becoming involved in the future. Bankers were quite reluctant to quantify the proportion of fixed-rate assets carried on their books, but in general it would appear that the amount of such loans for the typical Euro-bank is quite small.

4 Liability Management and Capital Adequacy

In addition to such traditional banking liability management challenges in the form of the appropriate mix of interest bearing deposits to stockholders funds and the correct balance of money market involvement, the Euro-bank faces the additional issue of virtually complete dependence for its liabilities on an interbank market which, as the events of 1974 have demonstrated, can be a highly volatile and uncertain source of funds. While the Euromarket loan pricing concept has simplified the banker's task of ensuring a relatively fixed gross interest margin on the bulk of his loan portfolio, a concept which does not exist in many national money markets, he cannot avoid the fact that he is essentially funding loans with an average life of perhaps three years with money market deposits of primarily three to six months in maturity.

Bank for International Settlements data perhaps best reflect the Euro-bank's almost complete dependence on interbank deposits as a source of funds. As of end-1974, only 14 per cent of reporting BIS countries' gross foreign currency liabilities were to non-bank institutions, down from 18 per cent in 1970.[1] The Eurocurrency sector is acknowledged to be largely an interbank market, but the proportion of non-bank deposits available to Euro-banks is significantly less than that provided to the large US and continental banks in their home offices and London branches. Some indication of this is found in the Bank of England statistics which are summarised in Table H.

In mid-1975, whereas the entire UK banking sector looked to the London interbank market for 21 per cent of its total sterling and foreign currency liabilities, consortium banks relied on the market for a total of 35 per cent of liabilities. In contrast, the London clearing banks were major net suppliers to the market, while their 20 per cent reliance on the interbank market by the American banks approximated the sectoral average. In the case of most Euro-banks, a significant portion of 'other source' liabilities represents deposit from banks outside the UK banking sector; unfortunately, no published breakdown of overseas deposits by type of depositor is available.

Behind this relatively low proportion of Euro-bank non-bank deposits lie such factors as the risk preference of major institutional and corporate depositors, the relative newness of most Euro-banks and the limited banking facilities they can offer to a corporate customer. The large

TABLE H

COMPOSITION OF UK BANKING SECTOR LIABILITIES AS OF 16 JULY 1975
(amounts in £1000m.)

	Total Liabilities[a]		of which:							
			Sterling				Foreign Currency			
			from UK Banking Sector		Other Sources[b]		from UK Banking Sector		Other Sources[b]	
	Amount	% of Sector	Amount	% of Total Sector	Amount	% of Total Sector	Amount	% of Total Sector	Amount	% of Total Sector
Total Banking Sector of which:	121.2	100	7.9	6.5	37.0	30.5	17.2	14.2	59.0	48.7
London Clearing Banks	26.6	21.9	.8	3.0	21.8	82.0	.8	3.0	3.1	11.7
Accepting Houses	4.9	4.0	.5	10.2	1.7	34.7	.7	14.3	2.0	40.8
American Banks	33.3	27.5	1.3	3.9	2.8	8.4	5.3	15.9	23.8	71.5
Japanese Banks	10.7	8.8	.2	1.9	.1	.9	3.0	28.0	7.5	70.1
Other Overseas Banks	19.3	15.9	.8	4.1	1.7	8.8	3.5	18.1	13.4	69.4
Consortium Banks	5.1	4.2	.2	3.9	.3	5.9	1.6	31.4	2.9	56.9

[a]Excluding items in suspense and transmission and capital and other funds.
[b]Includes Certificates of Deposit, some of which are held by other banks.
Source: Bank of England *Quarterly Bulletin*, vol. 15, no. 3 (Sep 1975) Table 8.

multinational client has traditionally banked abroad with the overseas branches of his lead bank at home and/or a major local — i.e. — UK bank for a variety of subjective and objective reasons. Such a corporation places a high premium on the safety of its surplus funds and has usually proven reluctant to place funds with a lesser known bank despite a marginal yield advantage. Even other financial institutions such as central banks, insurance companies, and pension funds tend to place funds with the largest and best established London banks rather than go through the administrative procedure of verifying the credit standing of a relatively new and smaller Euro-bank. Normal commercial banking services such as money transfer, letters of credit, collections, and checking and payroll accounts for employees are much more efficiently handled by the large staffs of the London branches of UK banks than by a Euro-bank with a bare bones operational staff. Finally, the personal contacts which often lie behind the choice of a new bank take time to develop, and most Euro-banks are too new in the market to have established many such relationships.

One of the products of dependence on interbank funds is an aggravation of the maturity mismatch which has naturally arisen as loan maturities have been extended to periods of ten years and more. A most useful indicator of the extent of final maturity mismatching is provided by Bank of England data which analyse the net position by final maturity of assets and liabilities for periods ranging from call to over three years. Table I provides a comparison of this maturity analysis for the UK foreign currency banking sector as a whole and for the category of consortium banks, which represent a major component of the Euro-banking community, for the period since data were initially accumulated in August 1974. The data are shown as the net borrowed (−) or lent) (+) position for the period expressed as a percentage of total liabilities to provide a proportional view of maturity mismatch. Maturities given are final, rather than roll-over period, maturities.

While both the industry and Euro-banks are net borrowers in the period from call to six months and generally lenders beyond this point, the net lending mismatch for Euro-banks is significantly larger than for the sector as a whole. In May 1975, for example, 27 per cent of the consortium banks' liabilities were represented by the excess of claims beyond three years over liabilities for the same period as opposed to only 13 per cent for the banking sector. These longer term claims, of course, generally represent the commitment period of a long-term loan priced on a roll-over basis. The relatively heavy mismatch for UK consortium banks in a sector already borrowing short and lending long probably reflects a combination of higher average life of loans and a relative lack of access to deposits of over three to six months.

The supply of interbank deposits thus available to Euro-banks fluctuates in size and character with the lending banks' posture towards

TABLE I
MATURITY ANALYSIS OF NET FOREIGN ASSETS AND LIABILITIES OF UK BANKS: NET POSITION FOR PERIOD AS % OF TOTAL LIABILITIES

| | Maturity Period | | | | | | | |
Date	Call to 8 Days Excl. C/Ds	Incl. C/Ds	8 Days to 1 Mtb	1 Mtb to 3 Mtbs	3 Mtbs to 6 Mtbs	6 Mtbs to 1 yr	1 yr to 3 yrs	Over 3 yrs
(1) OVERALL UK BANKING SECTOR								
30 Aug 1974	(4.4)	(2.4)	(2.7)	(3.5)	(1.8)	.6	3.4	8.4
29 Nov 1974	(4.8)	(2.7)	(3.6)	(4.1)	(1.8)	.4	3.3	10.5
19 Feb 1975	(5.5)	(3.5)	(2.9)	(5.1)	(2.6)	.2	3.9	12.7
21 May 1975	(6.7)	(4.5)	(2.1)	(4.2)	(2.6)	(.6)	3.7	13.2
(2) CONSORTIUM BANKS								
30 Aug 1974	(2.0)	3.6	(10.6)	(13.4)	(10.5)	1.4	11.4	24.3
29 Nov 1974	(6.9)	(1.1)	(11.7)	(15.2)	(7.9)	1.8	11.9	29.1
19 Feb 1975	(3.2)	.5	(11.2)	(16.4)	(8.5)	2.3	11.4	27.8
21 May 1975	(5.1)	(1.2)	(8.3)	(13.9)	(9.8)	.9	10.6	27.2

Source: Bank of England *Quarterly Bulletin*, vol. 15, no. 3 (Sep 1975) Table 22.

interbank assets, current level of risk preference and their source of funds, While the typical interbank deposit has a maturity of three, six or twelve months which corresponds to the standard rollover periods for Eurocurrency loans, much longer deposits are available periodically in the market with maturities of up to five years or more. These latter tend to be placed with large US, UK and European banks, and in moments of market nervousness are rarely offered to Euro-banks. The London branches of large American banks and other UK and Continental banks which are the largest net lenders to the Euro-banks are often influenced in their placing of deposits by home office policy. At the end of 1974, for example, when US banks were under pressure to reduce balance sheet growth, interbank assets placed in the Eurocurrency market in many cases were substantially reduced. During periods of market nervousness when there is significant pressure to take action against possible losses on interbank loans, extension of credit to smaller and newer banks tends to be the first to be cut back.

On the other hand, until mid-1974 these banks, in the context of building larger asset and earnings bases, were often prepared to lend on an interbank basis with relatively little financial analysis or personal knowledge of the borrowing bank and in amounts which bore little relationship to the latter's resources, on the implicit assumption that a participant in the market possessed sufficient capital resources, support from stockholders or a potential call on Central Bank assistance to be able to meet its obligations. A substantial portion of the interbank segment of the Eurocurrency market's growth in the early 1970s was undoubtedly due to the ease with which relative newcomers to the market could tap the market for substantial amounts without provoking the questions which would have been asked of a corporate borrower. While many banks had always done a conscientious job of analysing their interbank commitments, the failure of the US National Bank of San Diego in 1973 followed by that of Franklin National Bank and Bankhaus I.D. Herstatt in mid-1974 provoked a widespread and sudden awareness – and often exaggeration – of the risks in lending to any but the very largest and best banks in the international system.

The significance of the latter two failures went well beyond the actual losses suffered. Franklin's demise shook bankers' confidence in the safety of physical size; Franklin's assets of $5,000 million made it one of the top twenty American banks. While Herstatt had long had a reputation for heavy exchange dealing in relation to its capital, the German bank's failure focused attention on the intra-day risk of spot exchange transactions, which had been regarded by many bankers as virtually riskless. Millions of dollars were lost by banks which had delivered Deutsche Marks to Herstatt in the morning to be covered by an expected delivery of the cover in dollars in New York a few hours later – delivery which was never made because of the bank's closure before the New York opening.

Following a wave in the second half of 1974 of rumours about the real and presumed difficulties of the smaller and newer members of the fraternity, which included a large number of the Euro-banks under discussion, what appeared to be a balance between reckless growth and sheer unreason was reached in mid-1975. A few Euro-banks were obliged to sell significant amounts of assets to parent banks because of inability to fund themselves, and a much larger number had recourse to informal stockholder support through direct funding, but no Euro-banks in my sample were reported to have been unable to meet their interbank obligations. The upsets of 1974 have brought in their train greater personal contact between lenders and borrowers in the interbank market, a more structured decision making process with regard to the granting of interbank lines and a greater awareness on all sides of the limitations of reliance on the interbank market.

An understanding of the decision making process in the granting of interbank lines is thus critical to an appreciation of the liability management strategy of the Euro-bank. Technically, interbank lines are undisclosed and uncommitted internal guidance lines establishing the maximum amount and maturity of funds a bank may be prepared to lend another bank. Though theoretically undisclosed, most Euro-banks become reasonably well aware of the existence and often amount of these lines through observance of the deposits appearing — or not appearing — on their books and the informal market chatter which takes place with other bank dealers. A typical Euro-bank may have lines for several hundred other banks, which in itself represents a significant administrative burden. These banks are selected on the basis of presumed creditworthiness, personal and corporate relationships, the other bank's activity in the market, reciprocity in dealing, and the presence of other business relationships. Having determined from an analysis of these considerations that a line should be granted, management usually fixes the size of the line on the basis of the taking bank's capital.

Most Euro-banks interviewed in mid-1975 used 5—20 per cent of the borrower's net worth as a standard which could be adjusted up or down by special circumstances; a figure of 10 per cent was the one most often mentioned as a standard maximum. Smaller banks tend to establish a maximum absolute line they will grant of, say, up to $5 million, while many banks will not lend more than their capital to any other institution regardless of the latter's size and creditworthiness. Quite often borrowing banks will be split into two or more categories of creditworthiness; the top market category can be granted funds for up to twelve months or more, with three or six months being regarded as the maximum exposure for the lesser categories. Lines for spot and forward foreign exchange dealing may be granted almost automatically as a multiple of perhaps four times the deposit dealing lines, although some banks regard this as a completely separate management decision. A number of Euro-banks, in addition, establish a maximum daily delivery exposure combining both foreign exchange and deposit liabilities which will fix a maximum possible exposure to non-payment on any given day resulting from cumulative deposit and foreign exchange obligations outstanding on that day. In the case of many wholly-owned subsidiaries and a few consortium banks, the Euro-bank subsidiary is granted a portion of a global line established for the borrowing institutions by the parent or parents.

On the other hand, a relatively small number of Euro-banks still determine their interbank line exposure without fixed guidelines. To these banks more subjective factors such as personal relationships, usage by the other bank and reciprocity are the vital factors in establishing and modifying an interbank dealing relationship.

In particular since the formalisation of the interbank dealing decision making process which began in mid-1974, the management of most Euro-banks has devoted a significant amount of time to the task of establishing, restoring and possibly increasing the lines it is granted from other banks. Liability management has thus often become synonymous with the maintenance of one's market reputation and borrowing base provided by other bankers. In the greater era of frankness engendered by the problems of 1974 and the universal acknowledgment of dependence on the interbank market, the Euro-bank manager discusses more freely with potential lending banks his asset strategy, the degree of parent support and in particular any significant problems he may have in his loan portfolio. Euro-banks also are less hesitant about invoking overall relationships, including that of their parent institutions, to bring about the desired result of obtaining or retaining an interbank line.

One of the consequences of the sharpened perception of vulnerability to the vagaries of the interbank market has been the focus on parent bank support of their Euro-bank offspring. At their inception, most Euro-banks were provided with publicised or informal lines of credit, often a multiple of their capital funds, from parent institutions. In the turmoil of 1974, the adequacy of even this level of support was called into question, and in the context of an international Central Bank programme of delineation of responsiblity, the Bank of England in late 1974 requested and received letters of support from Euro-bank stockholders which implied a level of moral support going beyond their strictly legal commitments to a limited liability company. While most Euro-bankers considered such a letter an unnecessary restatement of the obvious, this action by the Bank of England in all likelihood contributed to a restoration of market confidence.

Another consequence of the events of 1974 for liability management has been the phenomenon of tiering, or differentiation of rates paid by different banks for interbank deposits. Whereas little if any differentiation in the London Interbank Offered Rate (LIBOR) was made previously among banks, the heightened sensitivity to relative creditworthiness created a situation in 1974 whereby certain categories of banks were expected to pay a premium over the offered rate whose level was dependent upon their presumed creditworthiness. Hence, 'Japanese', 'Italians', 'consortia' and 'small merchants' found themselves asked to pay a premium for funds which not only directly reduced their gross interest spread but also implicitly impugned their credit standing. The almost universal reaction among Euro-banks, which were among those most affected by the tiering of rates, was not to pay 'over the odds' on the reasonable assumption that such a concession would either confirm the lender's view of relative creditworthiness or lead to a higher premium being asked on the subsequent occasion — or both! As in the case of one's lending record, one's ability to resist paying a premium for funds became a symbol of manhood in the Euro-market, and there well may be a difference between the reality of rates paid and the claims of a bank's management anxious to confirm the bank's reputation. To the extent that funds have been declined by management because of the premium requested, Euro-banks have been forced to restrict asset growth, run involuntary deposit mismatch positions or call on parental assistance.

While the successive shocks administered in 1974 to the interbank market resulted in a salutory rationalisation of interbank lending practices and other positive benefits, it also pointed up the key role which confidence — and lack of it — plays in the Euromarket. The boom of 1972–3 with its sense of permanent upward momentum, large dealing positions and heavy volume almost overnight gave way to widespread gloom which envisaged not only the disappearance of many Euro-banks but also the possible drying up of the Euromarket or its replacement by a club of a few dozen of the largest banks who alone would be able to attract funds. In the event, a combination of good sense, action by the relevant authorities and the natural flow of funds from low to high yielding employment righted the ship in late 1974. While there is no assurance this confidence cycle will not be repeated, Euro-bank managements are now equipped with defensive techniques of liability management which should prove useful if the cycle should repeat itself.

The turmoil of 1974 also focused management attention on the desirability of greater reliance on customer deposits to diminish the absolute and relative dependence on the interbank market. With the exception of several Euro-banks who operate virtually as the London branch of their parents, these institutions as pointed out previously rarely have a significant natural customer deposit base. A fairly large minority of the Euro-banks interviewed expressed the view that building a customer deposit base was neither realistic nor particularly desirable in view of their inability to provide the facilities necessary to adequately service corporate or individual deposits, their parents' greater capabilities and presumed preference to handle this business themselves, and the greater inclination by these depositors since the events of 1974 for the safety of the very largest banks. Even if sizable customer deposits were obtained, these banks feel that their ultimate fate in a repetition of the 1974 crisis would still be in the hands of other banks as some degree of dependence on interbank funds will inevitably exist.

On the other hand, a majority of the banks interviewed placed a fairly high priority on building a customer deposit base despite the acknowledged difficulties for most banks in achieving any degree of success. Such banks pointed to the relative stability of these deposits, the ability in some cases to pay lower rates than in the interbank market because of close relationships or the relatively small size of individual deposits, and the cushion even a small portion of these deposits would provide in offsetting the fluctuations in sentiment and volume of the interbank market.

While no particularly useful published data are available, in practice the Euro-banks interviewed held in mid-1975 proportions of customer deposits which ranged from zero to over 60 per cent of total liabilities. The average bank characterised its customer proportion as 'very small', which appears in practice to approximate 10—20 per cent of the total. At the low end of the scale are some of the newest banks and those who make no effort to attract such deposits, while at the other extreme are the consortia and wholly-owned subsidiaries who function effectively as London branches of the parent organisation with a number of long standing customers of the parent who deposit regularly at the subsidiary bank, presumably with the active encouragement of the stockholder institutions. Banks with a regional character generally attract central bank and other funds, often in large amounts, from the particular region. Some of the larger and better established banks bid actively and successfully for deposits of large multinational corporations.

Banks with sectoral specialisation in energy and shipping also attract deposits from these sectors, with the latter able to command often substantial aggregate amounts through charter retention accounts in connection with secured loans outstanding. In most cases, deposits from customers of the parent banks provide a significant percentage of total non-interbank deposits, whereas the direct efforts of the Euro-bank itself to attract funds from depositors unconnected with the group have had limited success.

Another facet of liability management which received special attention during the 1974 crisis of confidence is the generally accepted principle that a Euro-bank must appear both as a lender and taker of interbank funds despite the general recognition of the low, if non-existent, profitability of interbank loans for these banks and their acknowledged net dependence on this source of funds. With a few exceptions in the form of banks who considered such a two-way activity to be purely cosmetic and unnecessary, all the banks interviewed expressed the view that an undefined and presumably flexible percentage of their borrowings should be relent in the interbank market. Apart from the understandable desire to provide balance sheet liquidity and balance and to maintain the professional objective of at least occasionally making two-way prices, those Euro-banks seemed to be responding to an often explicit criticism by the large net lenders that 'certain banks' were only takers and therefore not making a contribution to the market. The few banks who were prepared to quantify the relationship between interbank assets and interbank liabilities spoke in terms of 20–30 per cent of the latter being reinvested in the market. The view is often expressed that those banks which were active lenders as well as takers in the interbank market fared better during the 1974 funding crisis than those which simply funded their own loan portfolio.

As the preceding analysis indicates, funding a Euro-bank's loan portfolio and providing in addition funds for liquidity and/or interbank lending is almost invariably the principal mission of the bank's dealing room. In the case of a few wholly-owned subsidiaries, funding has actually been assigned to the local branch of the parent bank to minimise operating costs and obtain funds at the (presumably lower) parent's cost of money. In a somewhat larger number of cases, the chief executive has established funding as the sole objective of the dealing team with no expectation of profit from deposit dealing or foreign exchange operations or willingness to take the positions necessary to obtain such profits. Implicit in this position is the view that parent banks are better placed to take a view on deposit and exchange rates and that the Euro-bank's *raison d'etre* is making loans rather than speculating on interest and exchange rates.

In the great majority of the banks interviewed, however, the dealing room is expected to turn a gross profit before expenses in deposit dealing or foreign exchange trading or, in most cases, both. In a relatively small number of banks, in particular those with continental European patronage, maintaining dealing positions on which a profit was expected was regarded as a key element of the bank's strategy and a traditional aspect of international banking.

Recognising that profitability in a deposit or exchange dealing situation implies an interest rate or exchange rate risk, the majority of Euro-banks thus are prepared to take a view on the future of Eurocurrency interest and/or exchange rates in what they consider are reasonable amounts over reasonable periods of time. To a certain extent, this view may be the involuntary consequence of factors beyond the Euro-banks' control.

In the interbank deposit market, a matching deposit for a given loan may not be available in the right amount or at the right rate for several days following a loan rate fixing, and during periods of market stress as in 1974, involuntary mismatching was much more extensive. Correspondingly, in the exchange market, a counterpart for an exchange order executed on behalf of a good customer may not be available immediately so that a temporary exchange position may develop.

To a significant extent, however, voluntary positions are taken on the basis of a management view of interest rates or exchange movements. If a downward trend in interest rates is foreseen, a bank may fund a six month maturity roll-over loan with a one or three month deposit to benefit from the prospect of renewing the latter at a lower cost. In the exchange market, an outright forward position may be taken in anticipation of an exchange rate movement, or a swap effected to benefit from an expected movement in relative interest rates of two Eurocurrencies.

Of the Euro-banks which acknowledge a profit objective for their dealing rooms, a number feel very strongly that setting any explicit profit targets for dealing earnings (above and beyond the presumed loan spread over LIBOR and presumed earnings on invested capital) and exchange profits is mistaken in that it encourages dealers to take unnecessary risks to achieve the desired level of profits. Most dealers in the Euromarket, with some reason in the light of the losses which have taken place in recent years, are most reluctant to commit themselves in a planning context to anything more than a modest profit goal. Of the banks which were prepared to quantify their profit goals, a range of 1/8 per cent to 3/8 per cent minimum margin seemed to be anticipated on the interbank lending book as representing the profit from running a successful mismatch position as well as any earnings from matching deposits at a profit. As explained earlier, in mid-1975 significant matched profits on deposits were rare in view of the need by most Euro-banks to pay approximately the offered rate at which their loans were priced.

In the light of the massive acknowledged foreign exchange losses by some of the world's largest banks in recent years since the abandonment of fixed parities and the totally unexpected interest rate movements in major currencies during periods such as mid-1974, earning a dealing profit in the mid-1970s represents a major achievement. While, for example, one could conceive of at least a marginal profit being made on a deposit mismatch over an extended period of time due to the normal slant of a yield curve, a number of mechanistic or formula approaches on an *ex-post* basis over the last decade would have produced overall losses rather than the expected profit. It should be emphasised, however, that mismatch policy remains for most Euro-banks a subjective, unquantified decision making process.

Table J shows the result over an eleven year period ended in December 1974 of applying these different mechanistic approaches to obtaining a deposit mismatch profit; in each case a loss over the period would have been suffered from applying reasoning which would appear to make good intellectual sense.[2] While other mechanistic approaches might produce more profitable results, these results confirm the importance of a unique blend of market feel, practical experience and the use of current economic indicators on the part of the dealing team in obtaining successful results.

The difficulty of managing such positions is complicated by the fact that few chief executives of Euro-banks have an extensive background in the dealing function. Even if this were the case, instances of unauthorised dealing or even fraud in the case of non—Euro—banks in recent years have confounded some of the best personal and procedural monitoring systems.

As is generally recognised, a deposit mismatch position involves both a liquidity and a profit risk. The former would exist in the case of a 'normal'

TABLE J

ANNUAL AVERAGES OF MONTHLY MISMATCH PROFITS UNDER THREE FORMULA USED (%)

	Case 1	*Case 2*	*Case 3*
1964	0.123	(0.123)	0.000
1965	0.161	(0.161)	0.000
1966	0.061	(0.001)	0.000
1967	0.243	(0.245)	0.106
1968	0.120	(0.108)	0.000
1969	(0.769)	(0.599)	(0.065)
1970	0.036	0.046	(0.523)
1971	(0.724)	0.027	(0.459)
1972	(0.370)	0.361	(0.141)
1973	(0.575)	(0.036)	0.313
1974	(0.131)	(0.151)	0.114
AVERAGE	(0.166)	(0.090)	(0.059)

Notes:

Case 1 — Riding the yield curve
Continuous lending of three months deposits which are funded by one month deposits on the assumption that a normal mismatch over a sufficiently long period will produce a positive result because the three months deposit rate is regularly higher than the one month rate (.21 per cent over this period).

Case 2 — Playing the Averages
Assuming there is some normal or average level around which rates fluctuate, one runs a normal mismatch (lend three months against one month borrowings) when rates are significantly above the average (and should fall) and the converse when rates drop well below the average (and should rise). In this case, the eleven year historical average of 7.17 per cent for three month deposits was assumed to be the norm, and the trigger points for mismatch action were taken to be 8 per cent (above which a normal mismatch was run) and 6 per cent (below which the reverse was the case).

Case 3 — Play the Winners
On the assumption that most mismatch profits are made on major, prolonged interest rate swings, mismatch action is triggered in either direction when a sustained movement seems to be in progress. Such a trigger was taken to be a 1 per cent movement within three months; if such an upward movement occurred, a reverse mismatch (lending one month against three month deposit) would be instituted on the assumption the movement would continue, and vice versa, until rate movements no longer moved the trigger.

Source: *Euromoney* (June 1975). Courtesy of Eurocurrency Publications Limited.

mismatch whereby a given loan is funded by a shorter deposit which must be rolled over before maturity of the asset. The profit risk in such a case would be realised if interest rates were to rise, forcing the bank to pay a higher rate when the shorter deposit was renewed. To the extent that a deposit mismatch position is permitted, there is a fairly distinct split in philosophy. On the one hand, some chief executives control the position by close personal inspection of the daily liquidity position and maturity ladder and frequent consultation with the dealers without the use of formal numerical guidelines. These liquidity ladders list by time period total net cash flow, usually daily for the forthcoming week or fortnight followed by longer periods beyond this point. By inspection a dealer can determine the amount of funds necessary to cover a given negative position or put out in the market a projected surplus.

On the other hand, roughly half of the banks which authorise mismatch positions establish guidelines based on maximum quantitative exposure and duration of exposure. The former control is derived from the liquidity motive and relates to the theoretical need in an emergency to raise funds to cover a net borrowed position in a limited period of time. Several banks have in mind an amount, unrelated to capital or deposits, which they could borrow from the market or stockholders in an emergency; this amount places a theoretical ceiling on the mismatch position. Some banks express this amount in terms of available liquid resources, such as holdings of certificates of deposit or rediscountable assets which must cover a net borrowed position over a given period. Other banks set an absolute or relative amount, such as 10 per cent of deposits or a major fraction of their capital, which is to a certain extent an approximation of the funds they could obtain from the market in an emergency to cut out a borrowed position.

A relatively smaller number of banks limit the maximum period from the spot date that a mismatch can be run, such as three or six months, to protect primarily against the interest rate risk which is presumed to increase geometrically over time. Within this period, absolute or relative limits are often placed either on the cumulative mismatch — specifically net borrowed position — at any given date plus any period of a few weeks within that period which may have to be covered.

Foreign exchange activity may include relatively passive operations such as covering spot or forward exchange orders given by customers and generating a deposit for lending purposes in a given currency through a covered swap out of another currency. It also may involve spot-forward or forward-forward transactions for interest rate arbitrage purposes where the dealer anticipates a differential interest rate movement between the currencies. Finally, outright spot or forward positions may be taken when the dealer anticipates a differential movement in exchange rates. While usually pointing out that any such outright positions were relatively small and infrequent, roughly half of the banks running a dealing function were prepared to take such positions as of the summer of 1975. In only a small number of cases did the bank establish modest profit targets for the foreign exchange function, although most banks expected this function to turn at least a small profit before expenses.

For the banks which were prepared to take a position risk, a minority of chief executives use no guidelines for controlling the position but instead rely on close personal contact with the dealers, regular examination of actual spot and forward positions and direct instructions to take or cut out a position. The majority, however, use a fairly standard control format which places limits by each dealing currency on the spot open position, spot against overall forward position and individual open positions within the forward ladder. The latter control is considered desirable as an overall forward position may be balanced but contain within the maturity ladder an otherwise hidden contract to sell a currency on one forward date and buy it back on another, thereby exposing the bank to an exchange risk at the first maturity. An overall spot or forward maximum position for all currencies combined is often applied. In addition, a weighting system placing a higher weight over time may be used to limit forward-forward exposure. In the case of some wholly-owned subsidiaries which form part of a world-wide network, the parent home office establishes these guidelines on the basis of usage, the affiliate's track record and the parent's view of relative dealing capabilities. In some cases intra-day limits are imposed, but most banks control their spot and forward exposure on a close of business basis. While very few absolute limits were cited, those mentioned represented a fairly small percentage of capital funds — say $1–2 million for spot open positions by currency.

A significant source of exchange dealing profits for several Euro-banks is the making of a market in a secondary currency which happens to be that of one of its parent banks. By utilising their parent bank's dealing position in that currency as a counterpart and backstop, these banks are often the principal London market makers in currencies such as Italian lire, Swedish kroner, Spanish pesetas and Mexican pesos.

While available published information does not permit any serious analysis of the record of Euro-banks in achieving deposit mismatch and foreign exchange profits, the absence of any major publicised problems in this sector for Euro-banks and the willingness of most banks to continue these operations seems to indicate that experience has been reasonably successful. Most Eurobankers privately admit that mismatch results in 1974 were not particularly good due to the unexpected upward movement in dollar interest rates, but significant profits were generally made during the subsequent decline to mid–1975. Eurobankers note with a certain satisfaction that the well publicised foreign exchange losses due to fraud and unauthorised dealing occurred in the largest and presumably most experienced banks in the market rather than among the Euro-banks.

The adequacy of a Euro-bank's capital and the appropriate level of gearing (leverage) has been an issue which has aroused heated argument in the London market for several years. Gearing is defined here as total deposits divided by total capital funds, including subordinated debt and non-specific reserves. While no official published data exist, the sample of forty banks whose results are analysed in Chapter 6 had an arithmatic average gearing as of their fiscal 1974 year end of 13.2 times capital funds. This average, however, included several banks in the 19-22 range and a number with leverage of only 3–5 times capital. Euro-banks with relatively high ratios often point to the support of their parent institutions and in many respects consider themselves an extension of the financial resources of their much larger parents; others justify their higher ratios on the basis of the quality of their asset portfolio. While the older and larger banks tend to have higher ratios which were built up during a boom market period when funds availability was taken for granted and leverage was regarded less critically, many of the newer and smaller banks have found their growth automatically constrained by the market's unwillingness to extend interbank lines despite receipt of parent support letters by the Bank of England.

The actual size of total capital funds for the sample ranges from £1 million to £30 million with an arithmatic average of about £11 million. Included in this capital base is frequently found subordinated debt provided by stockholders; in large part as a result of market and Bank of England pressure, much of this subordinated debt has been converted to equity.

When questioned as to what they considered an appropriate leverage for their type of bank, most chief executives responded with specific figures ranging from 10:1 (usually reflecting legal limitations in their country of origin) to 25:1. Several were frank to admit that, given the nature of their business and the strength of their stockholders, they would strive to achieve as high a level of leverage as permitted by the market and Bank of England. Others were guided by what they felt to be the Bank of England's thinking as to the appropriate level for their particular institution. The ratio most frequently mentioned as appropriate in their view was 15:1. Chapter 6 provides more detail on actual Euro-banking gearing as well as comparisons with other banks.

A number of banks felt unable to express a view on a specific ratio either because such a view was considered irrelevant given the predominance of the Bank of England's opinion in the matter or the difficulty of distinguishing the Euro-bank from its parent's financial strength. It may be more than a coincidence that, with few exceptions, each banker set as a leverage target a figure somewhat in excess of his actual figure at end-1974.

The approach of the Bank of England to the issue of capital adequacy is outlined in a recent paper agreed between the Bank of England and the UK clearing banks.[3] This approach is essentially a flexible one involving an evaluation of the individual circumstances of each bank, its business and its management examined individually by Bank of England personnel over a period of time with the assistance of all available outside information. In recent years a continuous dialogue, intense at times, has taken place between Bank of England officials and individual Euro-banks which were regarded as having unduly high leverage on the basis of the Bank's analysis of the above factors. As outlined by the Bank in September 1975:

> it is recognised as inappropriate to attempt to quantify precise ratios between balance sheet aggregates; such quantification would lead to insufficient flexibility both between banks or categories of banks at any one time and for any particular bank in different circumstances. It should nevertheless be possible to develop over time broad numerical standards for the different groups of banks which may be used as yardsticks.[4]

While allowing for differences between different categories of banks and among banks within the same category, the Bank of England will be attempting to establish a relationship between deposit and acceptance liabilities on the one hand and free capital (defined as stockholders funds less fixed assets and other elements of a bank's infrastructure) on the other. In establishing an appropriate ratio, an attempt will be made to categorise various types of asset in terms of relative risk, and an evaluation will be made of the level of earnings as well as the record of a given bank's management.

5 Fee Earning and Other Activities

While a number of the earliest Euro-banks were established in the mid-1960s largely to participate in the medium-term lending function of the Eurocurrency market, several factors have led to an increasing focus on investment or merchant banking and related activities. American and Japanese commercial banks saw in the establishment of overseas subsidiaries a means of engaging in investment banking activities prohibited in their domestic markets. Other banks already carrying on such activities followed their clients into the international capital markets through their Euro-bank affiliates. An all-pervasive influence, however, has been the increasing awareness of most Euro-banks that income derived independently of a capital base was one of the few means by which a Euro-bank beset by rapidly rising costs of operation, limited lending spreads and a presumed leverage ceiling could produce a reasonably attractive return on stockholder funds.

One of the first and most logical merchant banking activities has been the management or co-management of syndicated Eurocurrency loans, an activity in which the Euro-bank can combine its balance sheet strength, financial packaging skills and marketing talents to earn management or front end fees. The size and frequency of these fees has been a function of market competitiveness and the attractions of the particular piece of business. During the borrower's market of 1973, a treasurer of a prime multinational corporation or a governor of a well-regarded Central Bank would become his own investment banker and bring together a willing group of lenders without anyone daring to suggest that a front end fee was appropriate. In contrast, during the lender's market of early 1975, management fees for less popular country credits rose to 1 per cent flat and more and were split among the originator, several co-managers who committed for a portion of the placement, and participants who simply signed on the dotted line. To varying degrees almost all Euro-banks have participated in the origination or placing of syndicated loans. Parent company customers and borrowers from the countries sponsoring particular Euro-banks represent the most logical candidates for loan origination. So-called market business, primarily foreign government or agency borrowers who come to the market frequently, represent a major target of opportunity for any Euro-banker prepared to travel to the borrower's capital, establish his credentials and make an underwriting or best efforts offer to place the borrower's next loan. To many government and official agency borrowers in the less developed countries with more or less permanent borrowing requirements, the principal considerations in choosing offers have been the relative attractiveness of term, amount and ability of the Euro-bank to produce results rather than any consideration of past or future relationship. In 1974 alone, for example, there were fifty different publicised loans for Brazilian borrowers alone, of which ten different loans were placed during the year for the central government or under its guarantee.[1]

Among the Euro-banks which took a leading role in syndication in the 1973—5 period have been the Euro-bank subsidiaries of large American banks with world-wide networks to generate and monitor business and substantial balance sheets enabling them to carry a large portion of the loan. Specialised London-based subsidiaries of these banks are primarily engaged in packaging and selling Eurocurrency loans; the bulk of their earnings is derived from fee income, as its share of the loan as a manager or co-manager is usually taken on the books of the larger parent organisation. Some major consortium Euro-banks have also been heavily engaged in managing loans, often committing firm for substantial amounts which could be taken by stockholder banks if unplaced outside the group. The placement process varies according to the size and complexity of the loan involved, but for a 'name' risk such as a well known government or agency hundreds of potential participating banks might be approached by telex and accept in principle by the same means. A Euro-bank's stockholders represent a natural source of placing power, although appetites of individual stockholder banks vary widely. A smaller or complex loan, however, might be discussed verbally with a limited number of potential participants prior to the sending of a telex or offering prospectus.

During the borrower's market preceding mid-1974, market conditions encouraged originating banks to commit firm for substantial amounts, often in excess of their capital, to secure a highly desired piece of business in the face of competition prepared to do the same. When the market broke in 1974, however, many large deals which carried pre-crisis pricing had to be held in portfolio with the result that funding problems were aggravated at a difficult moment and already narrow spreads were eroded by the tiering of LIBOR.

In the summer of 1975, the willingness of Euro-banks to underwrite an amount in excess of their intended ultimate participation was quite mixed. Somewhat over half of the banks polled were prepared to underwrite an amount in excess of that which they intended to take as a participant in the credit. In most cases, a multiple of two or three times the latter was considered a reasonable underwriting maximum. Quite often a substantial loan amount will be underwritten formally or informally by one or more stockholder banks along with the Euro-bank itself; such a decision would usually be taken at board level and might well involve as the borrower a customer of one of the stockholder banks. In other cases, a bank will either take market soundings on a 'no—name' basis or actually pre-place on a 'approval subject to documentation' basis with a number of other friendly banks.

The financial and visual benefits of originating a successful Euro-currency loan are obvious; the originating bank generally retains a portion of the management fee or override for itself as well as appearing as lead or agent bank in the publicity tombstone. For a bank unable or unwilling to originate business, a co-manager or sub-underwriting role can also bring a useful share of the management fee as well as a possible special bracket position in the tombstone. Unlike the Eurobond market, the unsold portion of the loan can be taken into portfolio without carrying the interest rate risk implicit in a fixed interest obligation.

A second major investment banking activity of many Euro-banks is participation in the Eurobond fixed rate publicly quoted securities and private placement markets. With an annual new issue volume which has ranged since 1968 from $3,000 million to $6,000 million,[2] the Eurobond market has been more volatile and smaller in volume of new issues than the Eurocurrency market but represents a major source of funds for certain major international borrowers. These tend to be prime, well-known government and corporate names with a credit rating superior to many borrowers in the Eurocurrency market. Underwriting and selling commissions are somewhat higher than is the case in the US.

The two key elements to a successful Eurobond operation are acknowledged to be good placing power in the sector of primary (new) issues and the ability to reduce one's portfolio to minimise losses if a secondary trading portfolio is maintained. There is relatively little institutional support compared with most large national bond markets, and ultimate holders tend to be largely individuals whose portfolios in many cases are managed for them by Swiss and other banks. Interest rate movements and investors' currency predilections tend to be major factors behind Eurobond price movements as opposed to underlying security values, as many investors use Eurobonds as a vehicle for taking a view on exchange and interest rates. The secondary market has been criticised for its thinness and inability to reflect these underlying security values.

The advent of floating currency rates has played a significant role in determining the character of the Eurobond market as well as its attractiveness to Euro-banks. When exchange rate uncertainty was added to interest rate volatility, the Eurobond market became less attractive as an investment market, and in the view of many observers both the primary and secondary markets, in which many Euro-banks participate, have suffered accordingly.

The Euro-banks interviewed split about equally between those who are active participants in at least one phase of the market and those who deliberately avoid any significant involvement. Those who participate range from banks who are active in all phases of origination, management, distribution and secondary market dealing to others who participate only as members of underwriting or selling groups or as secondary market traders. A number of Euro-banks, including both wholly-owned subsidiaries as well as consortia, point out that the Eurobond market represented their first objective and initial activity in London with Eurocurrency lending growing up subsequently. Those banks who have started from scratch in recent years in the Eurobond market have begun generally by building a secondary trading capability or by developing primary placing power and using either or both of these strengths to work into underwriting and selling groups.

Chief executives whose banks are active in the market emphasise the need to participate in capital as well as lending market activities to be able to offer a full range of investment and commercial banking services to their clients as well as to benefit themselves from the synergy between the two markets. Most participants acknowledge that their Eurobond activity is a service function and rarely provides a significant profit after all overhead costs are taken into consideration. In several cases it is clear that a parent bank places a high priority on participation, regardless of profitability, in the Eurobond market through its offspring. As in the case of Eurocurrency tombstones, the satisfaction of seeing one's subsidiary listed as an underwriter is a major motivation for many parent banks. On the other hand, those banks engaged in all facets of Eurobond activity regard the business as extremely profitable and express the view that such a comprehensive approach is the only one which ensures profitability.

Sharply different views exist on the merits of maintaining a secondary trading market in a specific number of outstanding issues. At least two of the banks in the sample have suffered highly publicised and substantial book losses on their dealing portfolio which went some way towards offsetting banking profits in the year the loss was taken. On the other hand, other banks have achieved regular profits from their trading portfolio in good as well as bad years, which they attribute to being willing and able to cut back their portfolio on short notice.

Placing power is universally regarded as the key ingredient without which a Eurobond operation is seriously prejudiced both in terms of vulnerability to adverse price movements and ability to gain admittance to underwriting syndicates. In developing their placing power, Euro-banks have solicited the traditional large takers of bonds such as the major Swiss banks as well as attempted to cultivate their own placing power, often with customers of the parent banks who had not previously been active as takers of Eurobonds. Parent banks who manage international portfolios have been of significant assistance in many cases to their Euro-bank affiliates by taking a good portion, if not all, of their allocation. In a few cases, Euro-banks themselves manage international portfolios which provide useful placing power.

Even if a bank develops its own placing capability and manages to avoid portfolio losses by rigidly controlling the size of its trading portfolio, it is recognised that the most attractive profits in the Eurobond business are derived from business origination. This sector, however, has traditionally been dominated by the major Wall Street investment banks, UK merchant banks and the principal continental mixed banks. To the extent that these institutions have an equity interest in a Euro-bank, some of the benefits may flow through to the latter in the form of a co-managership or underwriting group membership, but in many other instances, the Euro-bank has actually been excluded from Eurobond activity because of the presumed duplication of effort with the parent this might involve. The ties between investment banks and their clients have traditionally been strong, and the Euro-banks have not been able to penetrate this market through their lending muscle as they have in the Eurocurrency sector. Even the Euro-banks owned by the very largest American commercial banks have not been particularly successful in achieving significant managerships from the large corporate customers of these banks.

In explaining their reasoning, the roughly equal number of Euro-banks which have eschewed the Eurobond sector generally point to the difficulty of developing placing power in competition with several hundred other placers all marketing the same merchandise to a restricted number of takers. They are only too conscious of the impact on their profit and loss statement of a book portfolio loss suffered if interest rates turn unexpectedly upward. For a Euro-bank attempting to keep personnel and overhead costs to a minimum, the need to hire bond salesmen, dealers and administrative staff represents a significant incremental overhead which may or may not be justified by the eventual results. As a practical compromise with the objectives of their stockholders and their own understandable desire to appear as a co-manager or participant, several Euro-banks have participated passively in a handful of issues brought out by major clients of their parent banks without setting up a full-fledged Eurobond department.

A third general area of income generation is corporate financial services, which include a wide range of fee-earning activities: investment management, arranging back-to-back loans; project financing; leasing; new issues; mergers and acquisitions; private placements of fixed interest obligations; export financing; and advice on fund raising and corporate restructuring. The investment or merchant banking vocation of many Eurobankers, coupled with the obvious attractions of earning possibly substantial fees without burdening the balance sheet, have led many Euro-banks to undertake some sort of corporate finance activity. About half of the banks interviewed either had established a formal corporate finance function or had engaged informally in some type of financial service activity.

In setting up this activity, the banks have naturally focused on their functional and geographical strengths. Some banks with stockholders in the major world exporting countries have developed multinational export finance capabilities which enable the bank to put together extremely complex, multicurrency financing packages for their clients based on utilisation of the national export credit facilites of the OECD nations. Banks with parents in countries with active national stock markets often sell a securities portfolio management capability to individuals and institutions with specialization in these particular markets. In the same vein, a bank with strong regional connections usually offers a merger and acquistion service focussing on that specific region. Banks with energy expertise have put together major offshore oil field financings, arranged the sale of oil producing properties and advised customers on acquisition of North Sea acreage.

A number of other Euro-banks which currently have no corporate finance capability acknowledged that their institution must focus more on this type of fee-earning skill in the future even though they had not yet determined how to attack the problem. Behind this view lies not only the prospect of attractive profits but also a growing awareness of the need to differentiate themselves from other Euro-banks as well as the activities of those stockholders who are becoming increasingly active directly in the Eurocurrency market.

Success in the corporate finance sector for most Euro-banks to date has been relatively modest in terms both of profits and tangible results. A number of Euro-banks have successfully put together mergers and acquisitions for a fee, quite a number of complex projects have been structured, and investment management for a few banks probably produces reasonable profits. On balance, however, few chief executives indicated that corporate finance was now or likely in the near future to become a significant profit centre. In attempting to attract this business, Euro-banks are competing with national investment, merchant and mixed banks who have long standing and successful relationships with the corporate clients who are the logical candidates for their service. The success ratio of any merger-acquisition or project finance team is traditionally quite low in view of the number of obstacles to be cleared and the time and effort usually required to bring a deal to fruition. Perhaps equally important is the personal factor: a successful corporate finance executive is extremely well compensated and is naturally inclined to stay with a prestigious firm with a good reputation for corporate finance; attracting such an individual to an organisation with a predominantly banking orientation and compensation structure is a major task.

Another source of profits for a limited number of Euro-banks is the provision of such traditional commercial banking services as documentary credit financing and the operation of correspondent banking clearing accounts. These relatively labour-intensive activities have been avoided by most Euro-banks who consider themselves wholesale banks with a limited client base, but the experience of several banks indicates that these more traditional activities can produce a useful profit.

The final and perhaps most controversial activity of Euro-banks is the taking of equity stakes either on an outright basis or in the form of a sweetener or kicker to a loan. As indicated in Chapter 1, merchant banking historically has involved the investment of a portion of a bank's capital in trade and industry as well as providing the basis for lending business. By taking outright positions in commodities and project investments, banks like the Medici, Fugger, Barings and Rothschild probably produced useful trading profits to supplement their banking income. While the term 'merchant bank' is used rather loosely in the London market to cover anything from a pure Eurocurrency lending bank to an aggressive institution with a major share of its assets in equities and high risk loans, a few Euro-banks in the early 1970s did invest in quoted and unquoted UK and foreign securities and made loans which were acknowledged to carry a level of risk with which a commercial bank might feel uncomfortable. While the world's stock and real estate markets were buoyant, significant profits were made on security gains and the realisation of equity kickers where the Euro-bank had invested seed money or provided a tranche of subordinated debt. The downturn in the markets in 1974, coupled with the interbank crisis of confidence in the same year, reinforced each other in bringing management and stockholders to the tentative conclusion that taking substantial amounts of equity—type risks and funding one's assets almost entirely in the interbank market might be inconsistent.

Despite these events, a minority of Euro-bank chief executives in the summer of 1975 felt able to justify a strategy which included the taking a selected number of equity kickers in conjunction with their basic banking business. While most Euro-banks feel that obtaining an equity sweetener implies an unacceptable level of risk, a minority of bankers feel fully justified in asking for additional compensation in the form of a share in project earnings or residual value in connection with an extension of credit. Oil and shipping projects in the current market represent the principal vehicles for these sweeteners. In one case, a Euro-bank put together an oilfield financing which provided a percentage royalty to all lenders in addition to the usual interest compensation. Several banks lend to shipowners who provide such kickers as a share in profits, residual value or charter revenues as an inducement to make available terms, such as 100 per cent finance or lending on unchartered vessels, which do not fit standard commercial banking practice. Banks active in taking such sweeteners have found that only a relatively small number of these projects ever produce significant earnings to the bank and that the level of risk in retrospect often is greater that the lender had anticipated. On the other hand, the relatively exciting potential profits from this business continue to attract a limited number of banks interested in reinforcing their lending income and building on their specialist expertise.

6 Financial Performance

The financial performance of Euro-banks to date can perhaps best be evaluated by analysis of the published data of as large as possible a sample of Euro-banks for their fiscal years ended on or about December 1973 and 1974, the most recent period for which figures were available at the time of writing. To the author's knowledge, no official or private compilation of the earnings performance of Euro-banks has been made available publicly by regulatory authorities or private sources of information.

Fiscal 1973 and 1974 have been selected for analytical purposes in an effort to provide the most up-to-date results for a sufficiently large sample of Euro-banks. As 1974 can be considered to have been a unique period in the post-war history of international banking in view of the record loan losses suffered and the disruption of the money market, 1973 results have been included both to show recent trends as well as to provide a more representative time period. In view of the relative youth of most Euro-banks, the use of earlier financial periods than 1973 could severely limit the size of the sample used; for 1973, for example, eight of the forty banks reporting in 1974 did not exist, and seven banks in the 1973 sample were reporting results for the first time.

Subsequent tables in this Chapter provide key balance sheet and profitability data for a total of forty banks, all authorised by the Bank of England, which derive most if not all of their earnings from the Euromarkets and have a major operating presence in London. This list is identical to that of the sample of banks interviewed with the exception of one bank interviewed which does not publish detailed financial information, so that figures for another Euro-bank were substituted.

In structuring the sample, an effort has been made to include institutions whose age, size, sponsorship, range of activities and financial performance is reasonably representative of the Euro-bank sector as a whole. A number of caveats should be borne in mind in evaluating these figures. Banking disclosure under UK law is limited in a number of significant aspects. Published balance sheet and income statement detail is quite rudimentary. Banks are permitted to make undisclosed allocations to loss reserves, which may be taxed or not depending on the UK Inland Revenue's views as to whether a loss reserve can be justified by a specific likely loss, and a number of banks have established significant undisclosed reserves of both categories. Extremely little detail is given in individual financial statements; a breakdown of income and expense items is rarely available, and the key categories of loans and deposits are usually given as one line items with at most a breakdown between loans maturing in less than and over one year. While cash in bank and call or short-date loans are broken out as a one-line item, liquidity analysis is often hampered by the lumping together of other liquid assets with loans to banks of up to one year in maturity. On the basis of the publicly available information, however, Euro-bank financial performance can be analysed in terms of several key relationships:

(1) gearing (leverage) as measured by the ratios of deposits to capital funds and customer loans to capital funds. These data are given in Table K as of end 1973 and end 1974 for the sample banks reporting for these dates and broken down by number of years of operation. While more sophisticated techniques of leverage analysis exist, and the Bank of England as indicated previously has begun to refine the definition of 'stockholder funds', these ratios give a rough approximation of Euro-bank gearing.

(2) customer loans to deposits as an indication of the extent to which deposits are used to fund customer or interbank loans. Table L provides this data as at end 1973 and 1974.

(3) liquid assets as a percentage of deposits, as shown in Table M as at end 1973 and 1974, gives some indication of the short term liquid resources available to meet a deposit run off.

(4) profitability as measured by pre-tax profits as a percentage of stockholder funds and net income as a percentage of net assets is indicated in Table N. The pre-tax relationship excludes the variable of differential tax rates, while the net profits indicator represents a useful comparison in view of the wide range of individual gearing ratios.

In Tables K through N the following definitions are used:

Deposits include C/Ds or other obligations issued and may include a small amount of other liabilities if not broken out.

Stockholder funds include all subordinated debt provided by stockholders.

Customer loans include loans to local authorities and bills of exchange if broken out separately.

Liquid assets include cash and due from banks and discount houses (for periods of up to one month depending on auditing procedure), C/Ds (if broken out) and short-term liquid government securities (if broken out). Because of the significant variations in reporting practice, only tentative conclusions can be drawn from these data.

Pre-tax income includes interest paid on stockholder subordinated debt if provided separately but is net of additions to loan loss reserves apparently relating to that year.

Net income is taken before formation expenses and additions to contingency reserves which do not apparently relate to that year.

Average stockholder funds and total assets are derived, for the purpose of simplicity in calculation, by dividing the sum of the beginning and end year figures by two. Average data are used for 1974, but year end data are taken for 1973 because of limitations on available information. *Year end* is approximately 31 December; latest statement available is used, although no statement for a period ending subsequent to 30 June 1975 has been used. For banks completing their first full year of operations, period covered can range up to seventeen months.

Banks selected are listed in Appendix I and include authorised Euro-banks which are primarily UK companies but also include foreign Euro-banks whose London branches represent a major portion of total earnings and assets.

Number of years of operation represents period during which banks have operated in Eurocurrency market under their present structure; in many cases Euro-banks have been established in the past decade out of an entity which previously had no real international lending activity.

As indicated in Chapter 4, the level of gearing varies widely among Euro-banks and is clearly a key factor in evaluating performance. A variety of factors determine management or stockholders' attitudes toward gearing; these include the ability to attract incremental deposits from the market, evaluation of the risk component of a given loan portfolio, the views of the Bank of England, and of course the desire to maximise profits.

Table K provides gearing ratios at end 1973 and 1974 for the sample banks ranked by year of formation. Whereas the overall deposits: capital funds ratio has traditionally provided the most useful measure of bank leverage, the wide variations in the proportion of relatively riskless interbank deposits justifies the use of the customer loan: stockholders funds ratio which provides a better measure of asset risk as well as a better criterion for evaluating profitability in view of the low return on interbank assets. Between the two years most banks showed a decline in the deposits: capital funds ratio and an increase in the loans: capital funds indicator. Average deposits as a multiple of capital funds dropped from 16.4 in 1973 to 13.2 in 1974, while on average customer loans as a multiple of the same figure remained constant at 7.7 times. This phenomenon is probably attributable to a desire to reduce interbank loans rather than customer loans in the face of general pressure to cut overall gearing. The high and low extremes showed quite marked declines, as individual Euro-banks came under pressure from the Bank of England, stockholder and market forces as well to reduce their leverage. While many banks actually increased their gearing in 1974 over 1973, this was more than offset by the sharp decline in the case of several banks which had shown relatively high absolute ratios in 1973.

While the newer banks tend to be less highly geared than most, there is

TABLE K

GEARING (LEVERAGE) RATIOS FOR EURO-BANK SAMPLE AT YEAR-END
1973 AND 1974

Banks in Sample Classified by *Number of Years of Operation*	*Deposits as Multiple of Stockholder Funds*		*Customer Loans as Multiple of Stockholder Funds*	
	1973	*1974*	*1973*	*1974*
1 Year (7 in 1973, 8 in 1974)				
average	14.7	9.6	5.6	4.9
high	29.6	19.2	10.6	10.5
low	6.6	2.9	3.1	.8
2 Years (7 in 1973, 7 in 1974)				
average	16.0	14.5	8.5	7.8
high	22.8	18.3	17.5	12.0
low	6.1	10.8	3.4	4.2
3 Years (5 in 1973, 7 in 1974)				
average	18.6	14.3	11.7	9.6
high	32.8	20.9	26.6	19.1
low	11.1	7.6	4.6	4.4
4 Years (2 in 1973, 5 in 1974)				
average	18.6	14.9	9.5	10.7
high	19.5	21.6	11.2	20.6
low	17.6	6.4	7.7	5.2
5 Years (5 in 1973, 2 in 1974)				
average	14.1	17.4	7.0	9.4
high	16.5	18.0	9.4	10.1
low	11.2	16.7	3.8	8.6
6 Years (2 in 1973, 5 in 1974)				
average	20.1	12.9	9.9	7.4
high	21.4	14.6	9.9	10.0
low	18.7	10.3	9.9	4.0
7 Years (1 in 1973, 2 in 1974)				
average	16.6	11.1	n.a	3.6
high	16.6	18.5	n.a	3.6
low	16.6	3.7	n.a	3.6
Over 7 Years (3 in 1973, 4 in 1974)				
average	13.1	13.7	6.8	7.4
high	21.3	20.8	9.8	11.5
low	8.0	5.3	4.5	5.0
OVERALL AVERAGE	16.4	13.2	7.7	7.7
high	32.8	21.6	26.6	20.6
low	6.1	2.7	3.1	.8

not a very high correlation between number of years of operation and level
of gearing. There appears to be a tendency for gearing to rise during the
first few years of a Euro-bank's existence followed by a decline in later
years which may be caused by the three types of pressure mentioned
above. The range of gearing varies widely; high and low deposit:

stockholders funds figures for one year old banks were 29.6—6.6 and 19.2—2.9 in 1973 and 1974, respectively, while loans: stockholder funds multiples for the entire sample ranged from 26.6—3.1 and 20.6—.8, respectively.

A much higher degree of correlation exists between physical size and gearing. In 1974, for example, the two largest banks in terms of assets had deposits: stockholder funds ratios in excess of twenty times. For the thirteen banks with total assets in excess of £200 million at end—1974, the average deposits: stockholder funds ratio was 17.1:1, while for the sixteen banks with less than £100 million the corresponding ratio was 9.8:1, and the latter group included a large number of older banks.

Banks with the lowest levels of gearing tend to be the newer institutions, the smaller banks and those with either funding problems or a gearing ceiling imposed by home country regulatory authorities outside the UK. By the same token, the highest gearing levels tend to be shown by the largest institutions and a few medium-sized banks which had aggressively built up their asset base during their early years.

Another critical variable is the asset breakdown between customer loans and other assets, primarily interbank loans, as reflected in the ratio of customer loans to total deposits. As indicated earlier in Chapter 3, attitudes toward the composition of a Euro-bank's asset breakdown reflect such considerations as the desire to be seen as a significant lender as well as taker in the interbank market, the objective of maximisation of profits, the extent of attractive customer lending opportunities and attitudes towards liquidity management. Table L provides loan/deposit ratios for 1973 and 1974 for the sample banks.

Wide variations around the average 1974 loan/deposit ratio of 61 per cent were experienced, with a high of 102 per cent and low of 18 per cent. The banks at the high end of the scale were quite inactive in the interbank market, suffered liquidity problems, or expressed the view that redeposits in this market represented a relatively low priority compared with profit maximisation. On the other hand, banks with relatively low loan/deposit ratios included those making a conscious effort for liquidity and relationship purposes to redeposit a high proportion of interbank deposits, banks whose priority role in 1974 was to place surplus liquidity from their sponsoring country, and newer banks which were slowly building up their customer loan portfolios. The increase in the average ratio from 51 per cent to 61 per cent between 1973 and 1974 reflected primarily the movement into higher yielding customer loans in a context of pressure from various sources on total footings. Once again there is very little correlation between age of bank and level of loans: deposit ratio.

One of the most difficult relationships to analyse from published information is that of individual bank liquidity. While the Bank of England data on maturity mismatch shown in Chapter 4 provides a most useful indication of trends and levels of liquidity for different categories of

TABLE L

CUSTOMER LOANS AS PERCENTAGE OF DEPOSITS FOR
EURO-BANK SAMPLE AT YEAR-END 1973 AND 1974

Banks in Sample Classified by Number of Years of Operation	*Customer Loans as % of Deposits*	
	1973	*1974*
1 Year		
average	43	55
high	62	102
low	16	18
2 Years		
average	56	55
high	92	71
low	24	23
3 Years		
average	56	66
high	81	91
low	41	42
4 Years		
average	51	74
high	63	96
low	39	53
5 Years		
average	51	55
high	70	61
low	25	48
6 Years		
average	53	58
high	53	76
low	53	30
7 Years		
average	NA	98
high	NA	98
low	NA	98
Over 7 Years		
average	56	64
high	75	93
low	46	64
OVERALL AVERAGE	51	61
high	92	102
low	16	18

banks, the lack of detail in individual balance sheets for key short-term asset and liability items places real limitations on the conclusions which can be drawn from any statistical analysis. Assuming that assets available as a liquidity cushion include cash in bank, call loans to the money market, short term interbank deposits, certificates of deposit and other prime marketable, short-term obligations, it is possible in the case of most

Euro-banks to compute the relationship between these assets and total deposits as a rough measure of the bank's ability to realise assets to cover a liquidity gap.

While useful, it must also be borne in mind that any liquidity ratio is taken at the fiscal year end when window dressing — usually through matching short date interbank transactions — may camouflage a more normal liquidity ratio. Most importantly, only a running measure of a Euro-bank's overall mismatch position on a maturity basis as calculated by the Bank of England can truly reflect the day to day vulnerability of a Euro-bank to a crisis in which it could not renew its deposit liabilities. Needless to say, such data are not readily available.

In measuring a Euro-bank's liquidity exposure, the Bank of England would appear to relate a bank's standby lines of credit from stockholders and the market and its realisable short term assets to an arbitrary time period of several weeks or more which would give the bank, its stockholders and perhaps appropriate regulatory authorities sufficient time to work out a longer term solution to a liquidity crisis. As indicated by the nature of the 1974 crisis of confidence, traditional methods of liquidity measurement became somewhat less relevant in a market environment where a bank's presumed or actual difficulties can result in its name becoming unacceptable in the market within days with the resulting virtual impossibility of rolling over any of its interbank liabilities.

Table M provides an analysis at end 1973 and 1974 of the proportion of deposits held by sample banks in liquid assets. As the asset breakdowns published for individual banks are fragmentary and not always comparable, only limited conclusions can be drawn from the available data.

The most striking aspect of Table M is the extreme variations in liquidity among Euro-banks. While in both years the average percentage of deposits placed in liquid assets was 28 per cent, individual banks showed liquidity ratios as high as 59 per cent and 61 per cent and as low as 5 per cent and 1 per cent in 1973 and 1974, respectively. Once again, there is no real correlation between degree of liquidity and age of bank. Even allowing for the limited comparability of data, such a range seems to reflect totally disparate philosophies of asset and liability management.

Institutions with low liquidity tend to be banks who suffered acknowledged funding problems during the period as well as those, both consortium banks and wholly owned subsidiaries, who consider that their stockholders provide a sufficient liquidity backstop and believe that their primary objective is to run a customer loan portfolio rather than participate actively as a lender in the interbank market. Several banks with particularly high liquidity ratios are traditionally active as net lenders in the interbank market of funds derived from stockholders. In many cases, of course, year end ratios are far from typical of experience during the year because of the desire on the part of many banks to show a high proportion of presumably liquid assets on their balance sheet date.

TABLE M

LIQUID ASSETS OF SAMPLE BANKS AS PERCENTAGE OF
DEPOSITS

Banks in Sample Classified by Number of Years of Operation	*As of Year Ended Approx. 31 Dec*	
	1973	*1974*
1 Year		
average	37	38
high	59	61
low	5	2
2 Years		
average	32	31
high	54	60
low	13	4
3 Years		
average	24	32
high	50	59
low	5	3
4 Years		
average	17	15
high	21	29
low	13	1
5 Years		
average	28	22
high	46	27
low	10	17
6 Years		
average	19	29
high	20	48
low	18	13
7 Years		
average	30	19
high	30	21
low	30	16
Over 7 Years		
average	18	15
high	23	20
low	12	9
OVERALL AVERAGE	28	28
high	59	61
low	5	1

Profitability is acknowledged by senior Euro-bank management, with a limited number of exceptions, to be one of the principal objectives of a Euro-bank. In discussing the importance and measurement of profitability, most Euro-bank chief executives have in mind a specific pre- or post-tax return on stockholder funds as a reasonable long term target for their banks.

On the other hand, about one quarter of the chief executives felt that setting a profitability target was either impossible or irrelevant to the needs of the stockholder. In this category, several executives expressed the view that their realised return on invested funds was dependent on market and other forces, such as the Bank of England, which were beyond their control. Since these banks could not control such vital variables as spread and maturities (set by market forces) and gearing (set by market forces or by the influence of the Bank of England), establishing a fixed percentage return could, in the view of some managers, result in an arbitrary and possibly dangerous target; much better, in their view, to evaluate all Euro-banks on a relative performance basis. Another group of managers felt that their stockholders had established other priorities, such as obtaining an exposure to the Euromarkets or working together with a compatible group of banks, which were much more significant than even long-term return on invested funds.

For the great majority of Euro-bankers who expressed a view on a reasonable long-term earnings objective for their bank, the percentage returns (after 52 per cent UK corporation tax) indicated range from 7½ per cent to 20 per cent after tax on total stockholders' funds. The figure most often cited ranged from 10 per cent to 15 per cent after tax. In many cases, management felt an implicit or explicit pressure from their stockholders to exceed the return on capital achieved by the stockholders in their own banking businesses. Implicit in these targets is the gearing ratio they judged reasonable, which was discussed in more detail in Chapter 4.

Table N presents data for 1973 and 1974 for two measurements of profitability: pre-tax return on stockholder funds and net income as a percentage of total assets. The former reflects the traditional return on equity calculation; income is taken before tax to eliminate the impact of differential tax rates and before deduction of interest paid on stockholder subordinated debt in their capital structure. The measure of net income as a percentage of net assets is used primarily because of the wide variations in bank gearing which, if profitability is measured as return on stockholder funds, places the less highly geared banks at an obvious disadvantage. For both calculations for the year 1974, average stockholder funds and net assets are used as the denominator because of the frequency of sharp increases in these figures during the year; for 1973, however, data limitations required the use of end-year rather than average figures. Earnings for several banks in the sample are undoubtedly understated in view of the ability to transfer taxed or untaxed earnings on an undisclosed basis to hidden asset reserves. On the other hand, the pressure in most cases to report the maximum possible level of earnings for image and stockholder purposes — many banks have paid dividends in recent years — and the size of the sample should produce some reasonably valid results.

Pre-tax income as a percentage of stockholder funds rose slightly from

TABLE N

PROFITABILITY CALCULATIONS FOR SAMPLE BANKS, 1973 AND 1974

Banks Classified by Number of Years of Operation	Pre-tax Income as % of Stockholder Funds		Net Income as % of Total Assets	
	1973	1974	1973	1974
1 Year				
average	8.2	8.4	.20	.31
high	13.2	23.8	.28	.69
low	3.3	Loss	.12	Loss
2 Years				
average	16.6	15.7	.52	.45
high	39.5	27.6	.91	.79
low	5.6	Loss	.22	Loss
3 Years				
average	11.5	19.0	.21	.30
high	17.3	53.6	.26	.41
low	8.5	Loss	.18	Loss
4 Years				
average	15.9	15.8	.39	.28
high	16.7	27.4	.42	.51
low	15.1	5.8	.35	.03
5 Years				
average	15.7	19.7	.49	.38
high	29.6	21.5	1.08	.44
low	7.5	17.9	.18	.32
6 Years				
average	13.8	13.0	.20	.32
high	21.3	23.8	.35	.78
low	6.3	.5	.05	.05
7 Years				
average	15.3	14.1	.35	.21
high	15.3	21.3	.35	.33
low	15.3	6.9	.35	.08
Over 7 Years				
average	9.8	10.8	.33	.45
high	9.8	10.8	.53	.57
low	9.8	10.8	.33	Loss
OVERALL AVERAGE	13.2	14.3	.35	.33
high	39.5	53.6	1.08	.79
low	3.3	Loss	.05	Loss

Note: Banks with loss results excluded from calculations for years in which loss occurred.

13.2 per cent to 14.3 per cent between 1973 and 1974 despite the decline in gearing discussed previously. As could be expected, in both years banks reporting for their first year showed relatively low returns on capital in the region of 8 per cent although it is interesting to note that many of the older banks showed below average profitability. Some of the best average and individual results were obtained by banks in their second and third years of operation. The range between high and low profitability once again was extremely wide; in 1973, the high and low were 39.5 per cent and 3.3 per cent, respectively, while in 1974 results ranged from 53.6 per cent to losses on the part of four banks.

Not unexpectedly, there is a high correlation between gearing and return on stockholder funds. For example, in 1974 the fourteen banks with customer loans of less than six times capital funds showed an average pre-tax return on capital of 7.6 per cent, with the highest in this category achieving a 14 per cent return, while nine banks with ratio of 10:1 or more had an average return of 26.7 per cent. On the other hand, a number of banks with relatively low gearing were able to produce an above average return on stockholder funds by virtue of high fee income or other revenues not directly related to the size of their portfolios; this was true in the case of several banks owned by European institutions who passed commercial and investment banking business to their London affiliate.

The calculation of net income as a percentage of net assets eliminates to a large extent the impact of differential gearing. While pre-tax return rose in 1974, net income declined slightly from an average of .35 per cent to .33 per cent of assets between 1973 and 1974. Very little correlation between age of bank and net return was shown.

The peak return dropped significantly from 1.08 per cent to .79 per cent of assets in 1974, and five banks showed net losses as opposed to none in 1973. The lowest returns were shown by several banks in their first year of operations, institutions which suffered loan and security portfolio losses, and banks with relatively small customer loan portfolios. The highest returns appeared to be a function of management fees and corporate finance earnings, particularly by Euro-banks active in originating Eurocurrency loans; the subsidiaries of large US banks and a few European banks showed the highest returns on net assets largely because of this fee income.

In addition to gearing and the presence of significant fee or investment banking income, the level of loan loss reserves, both disclosed and hidden, and losses on securities holdings played a singificant role in the determination of profitability in 1974. Apart from one bank which reported a small start-up loss for its first year of operations, four banks reported net losses in 1974 which were due to substantial loan loss reserves established primarily against property loans. Other banks in 1974 showed book losses on fixed interest portfolios due to the decline in bond prices in 1974, while a large number of banks allocated a significant portion of earnings to specific or general loss reserves in view of the worldwide economic recession in general and conditions in specific sectors such as the US and UK property markets. On the other hand, several banks which held equity portfolios for their own account showed above average profitability in 1973 when world equity and real estate prices were booming. In many cases corresponding losses were shown on their portfolios in 1974.

Other less visible factors which may well have affected the results of individual banks are the level of operating costs and dealing profits, which cannot be determined from the limited published data. The cost of bank premises varies widely among Euro-banks; at one extreme are those with substantial amounts of prestige ground floor space in the City which may well have been fixed at the historical high level of up to £20 per square foot in 1972—3, whereas other banks have either benefitted from having fixed their rental cost at an earlier date or opted for less prestigious premises.

As discussed earlier, levels of staffing vary widely, and productivity can be assumed to show significant variations among different Euro-banks, in particular in high cost departments such as corporate finance or Eurobond operations which may not return a significant profit. Finally, results in deposit and exchange dealing probably had a significant impact on 1973—4 results for many banks. Given the wide swings in interest and exchange rates in this period, a bank which had a well-positioned mismatch book or took the correct view on major currencies could have added significantly to its overall results.

In terms of relative gearing, a recent study comparing the capital/deposit ratios of banks by nationality composing the world's 300 largest banks provides a useful standard against which to measure the level of Euro-bank gearing. Table O summarises these ratios for US, UK, Japanese and other banks for end-1974.

The average 7.6 per cent capital/deposit ratio ($1 \div$ deposit: capital ratio) for forty Euro-banks in 1974 approximates the 7.5 per cent and 6.5 per cent median figures for large US and UK banks for the same period and considerably exceeds the median figure for banks in other countries. The range of variation for Euro-bank gearing, however, is much wider than that for most national banks, with many Euro-banks attaining levels of gearing more in line with Continental and Japanese practice. Drawing strict parallels is not particularly useful, however, in view of the difficulty in comparing the different institutions. On the one hand, it can be argued that Euro-banks often have the support of major international parent banks and hold conservative, diversified loan portfolios; on the other hand, one can argue that parental support beyond the existing limited capital base is not necessarily assured, that future loss experience in the Euromarkets is likely to be much higher than in domestic markets, and that volatility of deposits in the Euro-markets requires a lower level of gearing.

A number of studies in recent years provide useful comparisons of Euro-bank profitability with that of national banking institutions. A useful study was made by the Federal Reserve Board of the 1972 results of American bank branches in London, which carry on a Eurocurrency lending business quite similar to that of the Euro-banks.[1] For fifteen US branches, the net after tax rate of return on total assets was only .12 per cent as opposed to a .54 per cent return on the banks' total domestic and

TABLE O

CAPITAL/DEPOSIT RATIOS IN
1974 FOR 300 LEADING
NATIONAL BANKS BY COUNTRY
OF DOMICILE (%)

United States		
	Median	7.5
	Upper Quartile	8.7
	Lower Quartile	6.3
Japan		
	Median	4.8
	Upper Quartile	6.0
	Lower Quartile	3.6
United Kingdom		
	Median	6.5
	Upper Quartile	7.7
	Lower Quartile	5.0
France		
	Median	2.9
Germany		
	Median	3.3
Italy		
	Median	2.4
Switzerland		
	Median	6.5
Netherlands		
	Median	3.7
Canada		
	Median	3.0
Other Developed Countries		
	Median	5.9
Less Developed Countries		
	Median	5.7

Source: Ian Peacock 'The Squeeze
on Capital Ratios', the *Banker
Magazine* (June 1975) p. 669.

foreign assets. However, by attributing earnings from imputed capital to these branches, this return, depending on the assumptions of gearing and yield on capital funds, could be more than doubled so as to approach the .33—.35 per cent average earned by Euro-banks in 1973—4.

A calculation of hypothetical return of a London-based Euro-bank made on the basis of 1972 yields and costs confirms the actual results shown by Euro-banks during the period 1973—4.[2] For a small sized bank (defined as one with a capital of $5 million and total footings of $100 million), pre-tax income was estimated at 14.5 per cent of stockholder funds, while net income as a percentage of assets was calculated at .36 per cent. For a medium sized Euro-bank with a capital of $ 25 million and footings of $500 million, the relevant figures for the model bank were

17.6 per cent and .44 per cent, respectively. These models assumed no loan loss provisions, an assumption which in many cases explains the disparity between these theoretical calculations and actual results.

A particularly relevant profitability comparison can be made with American banks, who are not only stockholders of a number of Euro-banks but also publish real earnings, unlike institutions in many other countries. Table P provides a comparison of the forty Euro-banks sample with a sixty bank sample of US institutions used by the First Boston Corporation.

TABLE P

COMPARISON OF EURO-BANK PERFORMANCE
WITH THAT OF SIXTY US BANKS

	Net Return on Total Assets	
Euro-bank Group	*1973*	*1974*
40 Euro-banks		
Mean	.35	.33
Decile 10 (Top 10%)	.94	.78
Decile 1 (Bottom 10%)	.10	Loss
60 US Banks		
Mean	.74	.65
Decile 10 (Top 10%)	1.07	.98
Decile 1 (Bottom 10%)	.43	.35

Note: US Banks are 60 quoted institutions in money
centres and geographic areas such as the Southwest,
Far West, Mid-West, South and Atlantic regions.
Source: First Boston Corporation, *Bank Market
Service*, vol. 1, no. 6 (6 Aug. 1975).

The average performance in terms of net return on assets in 1973 and 1974 of the Euro-banks was roughly one-half that of the American sample, with the top 10 per cent Euro-banks approaching the earnings level of their US equivalent. At the other end of the performance scale, however, the Euro-banks showed an even less impressive performance. It should be borne in mind, however, that the Euro-bank sample contains a large number of banks which have been in business only a few years, so that only limited conclusions can be drawn from Table P.

A broader comparison is shown in Table Q which provides 1973 and 1974 profitability data for thirty-six national banks located in six countries.

TABLE Q

ANALYSIS IN 1973–4: EURO-BANKS AND LARGE NATIONAL BANKS

Banks	Pre-tax Income as % of Stockholder Funds		Net Income as % of Total Assets	
	1973	1974	1973	1974
10 Largest US Banks				
average	19.2	22.0	.49	.51
high	26.1	30.4	.71	.71
low	13.8	16.1	.33	.36
8 Large Japanese Banks				
average	26.3	24.1	.42	.37
high	29.1	27.7	.48	.44
low	22.1	21.3	.38	.28
5 Large German Banks				
average	15.3	19.8	.23	.27
high	20.0	26.9	.29	.44
low	9.6	9.7	.06	.05
6 Large UK Banks				
average	25.4	22.3	.85	.54
high	30.0	34.9	.97	.73
low	20.3	14.1	.71	.35
4 Large French Banks				
average	31.5	24.0	.26	.29
high	62.2	34.5	.59	.53
low	13.0	16.6	.13	Loss
3 Large Italian Banks				
average	47.2	21.6	.06	.07
high	56.2	28.0	.07	.08
low	36.9	15.1	.04	.05
40 Euro-banks				
average	13.2	14.3	.35	.33
high	39.5	53.6	1.08	.79
low	3.3	Loss	.05	Loss

Source: *The Banker Research Unit.*

Note: The above comparison is of limited value because of the different accounting systems used in the various countries, the presence of variable amounts of hidden earnings, and the relative size and age of the national banks. Table Q does, however, place Euro-banks in a more favourable light than was the case in Table P. While Euro-banks reported on average a lower pre-tax profitability than any of the national averages, their net return was superior to that reported by Italian, German and French banks and not significantly below that shown by Japanese institutions.

7 Issues Arising from Euro-Bank Experience

In the decade since the first Euro-banks appeared in the mid-1960s, an almost unprecedented physical growth in a boom atmosphere through 1973 was checked by a chain of psychological and economic shocks administered in 1974 by a series of bank failures, the prospect of substantial international loan losses for the first time since the Second World War, and the world-wide tremors created by the shift in resources to the OPEC countries. Most Euro-banks have thus lived through periods of both boom and adversity, and, while many chapters in their history remain to be written, it is possible to identify in mid-1975 with greater precision the major unresolved issues confronted by these institutions.

With the wonderful gift of 20—20 hindsight, the Euroboom which existed until early or mid-1974 was a unique mixture of real economic growth, the evolution of a new international financial market structure and a self-perpetuating optimism in this market in which growth and expanding profits were almost taken for granted. On the asset side of the balance sheet the more passive of the Eurobankers could simply choose from the smorgasbord of syndicated offerings that arrived daily by telex on his desk, while the more aggressive could solicit business from a variety of borrowers throughout the world as well as develop the identity and expertise base which he felt was needed to differentiate his bank from his stockholders and other Euro-banks.

While new and untested borrowers appeared on their loan books, the outstanding post-war international loan loss record was maintained by steadily rising indices of business activity, increasing asset and stock market values, the willingness of new banks to take out existing lenders who were unhappy with the borrower, and amortisation schedules which did not particularly burden the early years of a credit. Increasing competition may have lowered loan spreads and lengthened maturities, but adding new loans had a positive impact in the short term on the profit and loss statement, especially if a front end fee could be booked when the loan went on the books.

On the liability side of the ledger, an often uncritical approach to the extension of interbank loans to new banks coupled with the rapid increase in the size of the interbank market meant that gearing levels could be increased significantly, availability of funds was often a secondary consideration, and there was little or no differentiation in the LIBOR rates paid by different banks. In this context there were few barriers to entry for a new Euro-bank. In London, Bank of England approval to deal in foreign currencies and deposits was granted to most banks sponsored by reputable banking institutions with at least several billion dollars of footings. Hiring key staff such as a competent chief dealer posed problems, but seconded personnel could often be used to set up the Euro-bank.

The events of 1974, however, produced in many respects the reverse of these boom conditions. Perhaps even more important than actual economic reality was the turnaround in market sentiment that at one point in the summer of 1974 threatened to jeopardise not only the viability of many Euro-banks but also the existence of the Eurocurrency market itself. Loan spreads of ¾ per cent and less for maturities of ten years or more now in the cold light of balance sheet and funding constraints lost their attractiveness. The threat of a world-wide depression and several individual country balance of payments problems made Euro-banks take a second look at countries like Italy which heretofore had borrowed at the primest of rates. Specific sectors which previously had been at the forefront of economic progress and the chosen area of specialisation of many Euro-banks suddenly turned sour; property companies in the UK, American REITs and VLCC tankers without reliable charters threatened real or potential losses. Sovereign risk loans to countries in Latin America, Africa and Asia which could not possibly rank very highly on anyone's weighted average of country risk looked somewhat less attractive. Bankers became aware of the vulnerability of the quality of their country loans to the willingness of other banks to continue to lend to these countries and the widespread domino effect of one country's inability to meet its Euromarket obligations on the credit of similar countries. Like the Euro-banks themselves, many of their borrowers would no longer be viable if a steady if not increased current of bank financing were not forthcoming to meet current obligations.

The impact of the change in sentiment was perhaps even more devastating on the other side of the balance sheet. The failures of US National of San Diego, Herstatt and Franklin shattered any implicit assumptions that interbank loans to all market participants were virtually riskless.

The reaction of many major lenders in the interbank market was a cutting or reduction of interbank dealing lines to smaller and newer banks. Such a reaction came close to creating a self-fulfilling prophecy by which otherwise viable banks would, in fact, become unable to meet their obligations because of a desire on the part of lending banks to cut their exposure to presumably weaker institutions. In view of their relative newness and smaller size, many Euro-banks were forced to fall back on a combination of parent funding support, reduction of interbank lending activity, or, in a few cases, actual sale of assets to parent banks. By early 1975, however, action by central banks such as the Bank of England as well as the passage of time without the feared collapse of a number of Euro-banks brought about the restoration of many interbank lines, an increase in volume, and a generally more optimistic mood in the interbank market.

With both Euro and other banks — particularly American — increasingly conscious of the limitations on their ultimate gearing placed on them by regulatory authorities and the market, Euro-banks turned to a significantly revised risk/reward ratio in their lending policy as one of the few means by which long term profitability could be increased. In a change in market sentiment reminiscent of the post-Penn Central mood in 1970, banks re-established minimum lending spreads and maximum maturity periods at levels reflecting a new lender's market, and credit quality reassumed its primacy in bankers' thinking.

In the cold light of post-Herstatt dawn, management behaviour during the boom period must be analysed in psychological as well as economic terms. Psychologically, new institutions and new bankers felt an understandable desire to build a performance record. In a market of over 300 institutions with highly similar objectives and lending criteria, the knowledge that a competitor was after a piece of apparently desirable business seemed in many cases sufficient justification to make an offer a 1/8 per cent lower in spread and a year longer in maturity. In a word, the herd instinct overcame legitimate concerns over risk/reward as bank after bank piled on a particular bandwagon. From an economic standpoint, pressures from stockholders and home offices to show increases in absolute earnings from Euro-dollar activities were reinforced by the good historical loss record since World War II and the apparent ease of making foreign exchange profits against fixed parities and mismatch profits by riding the yield curve. Return on capital was often regarded as a secondary consideration in the absence of pressure for a ceiling on leverage from regulatory authorities and the market itself.

From the turbulent events of the past few years, a number of unresolved issues have been posed for Euro-banks, while others have been resolved to a large extent. An effort has been made in the following analysis to focus on issues which relate primarily to Euro-banks as opposed to the Eurocurrency market as a whole, although admittedly the distinction must be an arbitrary one. One such generic issue not discussed, for example, is Eurocurrency loan pricing, which provides a theoretically assured gross margin but does not normally allow for such factors as changes in credit quality or the costs of doing business over a period of time which can exceed ten years.

One of the most significant of the unresolved issues relating to Euro-banks is that of loan quality and the Euro-banker's ability to evaluate a number of types of credit which are in many respects a product of the Eurocurrency market. Subsidiary to this overall issue are the ability to establish a reasonable loan loss reserve for international credits and the desirability of specialisation in some of the more popular types of geographic and sectoral loans. While other international banks confront the same issue in their sovereign risk and project lending, the relatively small size and lack of substantial retained earnings of Euro-banks coupled with their concentration on these credits makes the issue a particularly acute one for Euro-banks.

The difficulty of evaluating country risk and of dealing with sovereign governments has been well described in recent publications by such prominent bankers as Alexander Wolfe Jr[1] and Richard Cummings.[2] In brief, Euro-banks are lending in unprecedented amounts, for unprecedented maturities, to a wide variety of countries which carry a significant economic and/or political risk. The precedents from the nineteenth and early twentieth centuries cited in Chapter 1, when private investors' funds rather than bank deposits were at risk, are not particularly encouraging. Violent price fluctuations in a few key commodities, war and civil strife and a change in form of government lead the banking historian to conclude that some country defaults are inevitable over the period of time today's 'medium-term' loans to sovereign borrowers tend to be outstanding.

Even if one's ability to evaluate sovereign risk credits were better than the current state of the art, the length of today's maturities substantially limits the flexibility which banks like Barings had in the nineteenth century when short-term facilities could be run down when trouble appeared on the horizon. Confronted with a sovereign borrower unwilling or unable to meet its obligations, the banker's best course of action is likely to be to negotiate for the best work-out possible. While most if not all of these borrowers value highly their credit rating and will make every effort to avoid a default situation, history has shown how vulnerable these intentions can be in a time of economic or political difficulty.

World Bank statistics on multilateral renegotiations of debt owed to government entities show that nine countries, among whom five are active current borrowers in the Eurocurrency market, were obliged to reschedule $7,000 million in obligations in the 1956—73 period.[3] No similar data are available on obligations to private lenders such as international banks, but bankers often argue with some logic that their debt will be the last to suffer in a rescheduling exercise in view of the value attached to credibility in the international private financial markets. While rescheduling of their obligations may take place, banks understandably regard such a maturity extension with less trepidation than the prospect of partial or total loss of principal lent to a failed private corporation or project which is not associated with the sovereign state's ability and motivation to resume its role as a borrower in the Eurocurrency market.

A severe complication in evaluating country risk is posed, however, by the discontinuities produced by market psychology — some would say herd instinct. Rightly or wrongly, a major borrower or type of borrower can become unacceptable almost overnight in the Euromarkets. Italy, for example, moved in mid-1974 from the status of a borrower enjoying the very finest terms to one where, for various reasons, the entire market seemed to be 'full up' on Italy, with the result that official bilateral assistance became necessary. Following the heavy country borrowings of the early 1970s, a large number of less developed nations are now dependent on the Euromarkets to roll over existing obligations, and a variety of events, including the default of an entirely unrelated country borrower which shakes market confidence in a certain type of country credit, can result in the same type of problem faced by a Euro-bank whose market lines are cut. While central bank and official support may also be forthcoming in this type of situation, competition has eroded the leadership obligations which in the past would have enabled a traditional banker to a certain country to bring together a rescue syndicate if his client were in temporary difficulties.

Risk evaluation in private sector credits is equally if not more difficult. Although many bankers sincerely prefer corporate or project credits which can be better evaluated in terms of their professional training than a sovereign risk, the uncertainties for the former type of financing resulting from inflation, the size and complexity of many modern projects and changes in technology have been well described by Professor Charles Williams and others.[4] Such imponderables as the supply and demand for large oil tankers and semi-submersible oil rigs, the technological uncertainties of nuclear power and liquid natural gas systems, and the evaluation of oil under the North Sea represent levels of uncertainty reminiscent of the railway financing boom of the mid-nineteenth century which produced its share of massive cost overruns, over supply of facilities and proliferation of uneconomic projects.

Even in more traditional sectors such as real estate lending, Euro-banks have undertaken risks of which in many cases they were unaware. As mentioned earlier, significant losses have been suffered in the United Kingdom property market by Euro-banks who were aware that property values could fall as well as rise but who never foresaw the virtual disappearance for a protracted period of time in 1974—5 of the institutional market for real estate upon which so many deficit cash flow property companies relied to meet their obligations. Euro-banks have also been significant lenders to the much criticised US Real Estate Investment Trusts. While in retrospect much of this lending is subject to criticism, the number of bankers who correctly foresaw in 1972—3 the virtually complete collapse of this widely heralded new sector in 1974—5 were thin on the ground at the time. In oil tanker finance, which has also attracted Euro-bank interest, critics of the enthusiasm of bankers for a glamorous new industry which was over-expanding to meet a generally agreed level of demand should also bear in mind the almost totally unexpected impact on this demand of the October War in 1973 with its fivefold increase in oil prices.

For the majority of Euro-banks, the good old days when international lending involved self-liquidating trade finance or loans to the overseas subsidiaries of well-established multinational companies are well and truly gone. Building and maintaining a Euroloan portfolio in large part from market sources therefore involves some exposure to a combination of sovereign and corporate/project risk which has few historical precedents.

One hesitates to draw any historical parallels with earlier periods of international banking expansion in view of the obvious differences in environment, but there are some definite parallels in sovereign risk and project lending. The Medici with Yorkist English monarchs and the Duke of Burgundy, the Fugger vis-a-vis the Habsburgs, and nineteenth century French and English merchant banks with various sovereigns in Egypt, Turkey, Southern Europe and Latin America all at one time or another came up against a sovereign authority who could not or would not meet its obligations. While investors rather than bank resources usually suffered the loss in the nineteenth century, the number of new international banks who disappeared within a few years of their opening for business is, unfortunately, rather high.

From this issue stems the problem of establishing an adequate loan loss reserve. For the reasons given above, individual or industry-wide data provide little useful guidance. With very few exceptions, the forty Euro-banks analysed in Chapter 6 give no indication of total loan loss experience. Bankers' natural reluctance to talk about their less successful loans plus the paucity of reporting requirements for Euro-banks reduces one to analysing the occasional publicly available statistics which provide outstandings to a given troubled country borrower or the aggregate amount of a certain sector's borrowing in the London market.

For fiscal 1974, only a handful of banks in the statistical sample reviewed in the previous chapter revealed an allocation of specific amounts of 1974 earnings to loan loss reserves. In one case, the reserve approximated the bank's capital, while in two cases the banks' auditors felt unable to comment on the adequacy of the reserve established. In several instances, audited reports revealed the transfers of loans to parent institutions. As indicated in Chapter 3, many Eurobankers feel unable for various reasons to set a target loan loss reserve for internal management purposes. While those venturing to establish such a target have widely varying percentages in mind, the figure of 1½ per cent of loan volume often cited significantly exceeds the 1 per cent level regarded as reasonable for the US banking industry as a whole.

At the industry level, the Bank of England provides figures for the total exposure of UK banks to individual countries which would be of use to measure relative risk in the event of a country default or renegotiation. However, evaluating the ultimate loss from such an action and allocating it among the various sectors of the London international banking community is a hazardous task at best. The same is true in the case of UK property loans; Euro-banks participated to an unknown extent in the

£2,800 million of loans outstanding at end-1974 to this troubled industry.[5] From World Bank data it is possible to determine that $ 300 million in publicly announced Eurocurrency credits were made available to Real Estate Investment Trusts in 1973; this figure surely understates to a large extent the total exposure of the London market to this sector. In the absence of additional data, however, the only conclusion one can tentatively draw is that a large number, if not majority of Euro-banks have participated in loans to one or more REITs. Even more fragmentary data are available on the extent of Eurocurrency loans to owners of VLCC and ULCC oil tankers, and strong disagreement exists within the international banking community as to the extent of loss likely to be realised on these loans.

Another sub-issue which arises from the general problem of risk evaluation is the dilemma of diversification of risk as opposed to specialisation. The interviews reported in Chapter 3 bring out the importance most Euro-banks place on diversification. Asset controls based on country exposure, percentage of capital funds lent to a single borrower and ceilings on industry exposure play a key role in the asset management policy of most Euro-banks. In many cases, Euro-bank management seeks to involve stockholders in asset diversification decisions. Eurobankers in mid-1975 were well aware that a great majority of the recent international bank failures and substantial loan losses have occurred as a result of overconcentration on specific sectors such as real estate.

A contrary view, however, holds that a reasonable degree of asset specialisation is vital to the success of a Euro-bank. The natural proponents of this view are the Euro-banks whose sponsorship involves an inevitable degree of geographic or functional asset concentration. While offering their sponsors and the market the traditional advantages of specialist expertise, these banks generally regard themselves as extensions of their much larger parents and therefore able to minimise the disadvantages of overconcentration by support from financially powerful stockholders. On a more general plane, it is agreed by many Euro-bank executives that their banks can succeed in the long run only by establishing an identity distinct from their parents and other banks, and that developing specialist skills in financing growing and creditworthy market sectors is one of the few means of achieving this identity. In many cases, such skills are a natural concomitant of the Euro-bank's management team or its stockholder connections and resources. Rather than allocate their loan portfolio to dozens of different countries whose creditworthiness they feel they can never properly evaluate or to lend to industries with which they have no real familiarity, some Euro-banks prefer to focus on sectors which may carry a high perceived level of risk or complexity but one which the banker not only feels capable of evaluating and limiting but also receives more than adequate compensation in terms of fees, deposits, loan spreads and possibly equity kickers. Unfortunately, many of the sectors in the early 1970s which attracted this strategic thinking — shipping, natural resources, real estate, and energy — suffered in 1974—5 from overcapacity, economic problems and various uncertainties, so that many Euro-banks found themselves in 1975 dismantling newly established specialist lending units.

The second major unresolved issue for Euro-banks today is the adequacy of funding sources. The theoretical problem of converting short-term deposits into financial commitments of several years or more became a very real one in the second half of 1974. The fact that Euro-banks met their obligations under extremely difficult conditions is a tribute to intelligent central bank leadership, the willingness of parent banks to provide support in a variety of forms, and persistent efforts by bankers on a personal level to modify and rationalise some of the more drastic measures taken initially by the senior management of lending banks concerned about their interbank exposure.

Success in surmounting the 1974 crisis of confidence, however, provides no assurance that a similar or more serious one in the future, perhaps accompanied more by serious loan losses rather than the spate of rumours which was often the case in 1974, will not recur. Channels of assistance from parent institutions have been established if not actually utilised, serious attempts are being made by many Euro-banks to diversify their sources of funds, and personal contacts and structures have been established by individual managements and dealers which should prove useful in a future funding crisis. On the other hand, the ability of a separately capitalised bank to consistently attract interbank deposits to fund long-term commitments has been called into question. Rightly or wrongly, sponsorship or ownership in 1974 and 1975 has played a key role in a Euro-bank's ability to attract funds.

To the extent that a Euro-bank is unable or unwilling for strategic purposes to rely on parent bank funding, its management must continue to resort to the traditional methods of increasing the proportion of liquid reserves, reducing maturity periods and developing non-bank sources of deposits to defend against a future crisis of confidence in the interbank market. In the light of the 1974 experience, funding has assumed a priority in management thinking which will not disappear overnight.

A third unresolved issue is the Euro-banks' ability to earn a rate of return considered satisfactory by management and stockholders after deducting a reasonable loan loss reserve and assuming a generally acceptable level of gearing. Many Euro-banks have not been in existence long enough for one to draw any legitimate conclusions as to their long term profitability, but a return on assets in the range of .25 per cent—.40 per cent does not compare favourably with that of national banks in domestic markets such as the US, UK and several European countries. Return on equity comparisons are made difficult by wide variations in Euro-bank gearing, but if one assumes that the average gearing of thirteen times for 1974 represents a valid average measure of loan portfolio quality, management strength and other relevant factors, the realised 1974 average pre-tax return of 14 per cent on net worth in a sample which includes a large number of mature institutions would not seem to indicate that the typical Euro-bank will outperform its stockholders on this comparison.

On an individual basis, however, Euro-banks have and will continue to earn relatively high returns on capital and assets. In some instances, profitability is secondary in the minds of stockholders to such considerations as providing a useful introduction to the Euromarkets, developing specialist contacts and expertise, association with a compatible group of banks, and attracting or placing funds to and from individual sponsoring countries or regions. Finally, for the large number of banks in the sample established in the past few years, insufficient time has passed to permit the Euro-bank in question to develop its full profit potential.

What is clear on the basis of the evidence to date, however, is that Euro-banks have a major challenge before them to achieve a level of profitability comparable with that prevalent in major national banking markets. Inflating costs of operation, the prospect of loan losses which may well represent a higher proportion of outstandings than in the case of domestic lending, the relative absence of the cheaper demand deposits of traditional customers, and a loan pricing formula which places an effective ceiling on portfolio return for an extended commitment period will continue to restrain Euro-bank profitability. In view of the uncertainty of the loan loss outlook, it is possible to argue that the ultimate profitability of Euro-banks will only emerge over the next decade as today's loans mature. The increasing emphasis on fee income discussed in Chapter 5 is one response to this challenge.

Another issue for Euro-banks and their stockholders emerging from the three problems discussed above is the question of contingent responsibility of stockholder institutions. One must assume that in many, if not most instances, a separately capitalised vehicle was chosen to limit the stockholders' liability. The letters of support received by the Bank of England from Euro-bank stockholders in late 1974 and early 1975, however, represent a type of moral commitment which, particularly when provided by a banking institution with a world-wide reputation to protect, can be considered to go beyond that of a stockholder in a limited liability company. In practice, the funding support provided their Euro-bank subsidiaries during the 1974 confidence crisis was indicative of this level of involvement. The purchase of a Euro-bank's assets by stockholders occured several times in 1974 when the Euro-bank was unable to obtain funds from the market to support its portfolio, and similar asset support in the event of substantial losses is not inconceivable if the stockholders decide to maintain their subsidiaries' net worth at the expense of taking some bad loans into their own portfolio or otherwise subsidising their affiliate. One of the early precedents for this type of situation arose in

1970 when the United California Bank paid off depositors of its 52 per cent-owned Swiss subsidiary to protect its name despite the threat of stockholder suits against the US parent.

In this context, one can legitimately question whether a separately capitalised vehicle provides many of the legal advantages normally associated with a limited liability company. On the other hand, this objective may be relatively unimportant to most stockholders, in particular those owning consortium banks where a separate corporation is the only legal means of carrying out the stockholders' objectives. In addition, for American, Japanese and other banks who are legally prohibited from carrying on investment banking activities in their domestic market, a separately incorporated vehicle is absolutely necessary. The problem is presumably most acute for stockholder banks which are relatively small in comparison with the assets represented by their percentage stake in a Euro-bank which they may conceivably be asked to support by assuming assets or providing funding.

A final unresolved issue is whether Euro-banks are capable of generating the investment banking or fee-based income which many bankers feel is necessary to provide an attractive rate of return, establish a distinctive identity for themselves as an international merchant bank, or achieve other agreed objectives. The great majority of Euro-banks are owned by commercial banks, and with few exceptions top management has a commercial banking background which is not necesarily the best training for the capital market and corporate finance activities which generate a significant amount of fee income. As discussed in Chapter 5, some of the most profitable aspects of investment banking — origination and corporate financial services — are dominated by a limited number of well-established national merchant or investment banks, and relatively few Euro-banks are likely to displace these traditional relationships. To date the banks which have been particularly successful in generating fee income either benefit from business obtained with the assistance of stockholders who carry on an active investment banking business or, in a limited number of instances, have engaged a highly experienced team of investment bankers at some cost to break into this type of business. In most instances, however, one has the impression that relatively few Euro-banks will derive significant profits from corporate financial services and capital market operations. For many of the remainder, the management and co-management of syndicated Eurocurrency loans will provide the bulk of their fee income.

Before concluding this chapter, it might be useful to mention a few issues which appear to have been successfully resolved by Euro-banks in recent years.

Perhaps most importantly, Euro-banks seem to have successfully managed their deposit mismatch and foreign exchange positions during extraordinarily difficult periods of sharply fluctuating interest rates and exchange parities. The concern has often been expressed that bankers,

TABLE R

BANKING LOSSES ($m., financial year 1974)

Name of bank	Assets less Contra Accounts	Losses	Cause
Chase Manhattan	41,143	29	Overvaluation of bond trading portfolio
Crédit Lyonnais	32,723	38	Operating loss (after tax)
Manufacturers Hanover	25,754	30(P)	Charge-off of loan to Franklin National Bank
Westdeutsche Landesbank Girozentrale	23,649	114	Foreign exchange dealings
Lloyds Bank	21,021	77	Foreign exchange losses at Lloyds Bank International's Lugano branch
Continental Illinois	19,526	12(P)	Provision against losses at London merchant banking subsidiary, Continental Illinois Limited
Swiss Bank Corporation	16,401	NA	Dealings with Sindona group of companies
Union Bank of Switzerland	12,281	56	Foreign exchange dealings
Hessische Landesbank Girozentrale	13,323	717(E)	Investment losses, including large losses incurred through subsidiary company Investitions und Handelsbank
Norddeutsche Landesbank Girozentrale	11,336	127(E)	Investment losses, including those on loans to Rollei company
First National Bank of Boston	8,536	9	Cost of closing uncompleted foreign exchange deals arising from closure of Banque de Financement
Banque de Bruxelles	7,496	100	Foreign exchange dealings
Franklin National Bank	4,928*	370(E)	Foreign exchange and loan losses
Grindlays	3,732	21(P)	Provision against investment losses, including $33 m. provision at merchant banking subsidiary, Brandts ($16 m. of the Brandts' provision is for possible losses on property loans). (The Grindlays' figure includes a $5 m. tax charge on operating profits)
United Dominions Trust	3,322	61(P)	Provision against property loans
		22	Operating loss (including $3 m. tax charge)
Hill Samuel	2,729	10	Write-off of 50% of uncompleted foreign exchange deals left after closure of Bankhaus I. D. Herstatt
Security National Bank	1,803*	140(E)	Investment losses

Notes: Figures in local currency converted at exchange rates prevailing early May. Loss figures are given before tax unless otherwise stated.
*These banks have now been taken over by other banks and so do not appear in this year's ranking.
(P) denotes a provision against possible losses.
(E) denotes an estimate of possible losses.
Source: *Banker* (June 1975).

particularly the newer breed of Eurobankers, were vulnerable to serious miscalculation in forecasting interest and exchange rates which larger and more experienced banks often got wrong. In the event, it has been the bigger national banks who have announced massive exchange losses either through unauthorised dealing or a major position turning sour. Table R, taken from the *Banker* magazine, lists some of these and other publicised banking losses during 1974; in only one of these situations was a Euro-bank directly involved.

This relatively good performance would appear to stem from a combination of relatively small size, simplicity of operation and the awareness by management that a major mismatch or exchange loss could not be tolerated given the small size of their earnings base. With few exceptions, the chief executives interviewed regard the taking of significant deposit, mismatch and exchange positions as having a low priority compared to loan income and fees earned. This does not imply, of course, that Eurobankers have outperformed their more established competitors in money dealing operations, but rather that they are generally not prepared to take significant dealing risks and that control of a dealing room is simpler in a smaller organisation.

Another problem with which most Euro-banks seem to have successfully dealt is the tiering, or splitting of LIBOR paid by various banks on the basis of presumed credit standing. In the context of 1974 of emphasis on credit quality, various levels of premia over LIBOR were paid by a number of Euro-banks, and the concern was expressed that this would become a permanent pricing mechanism which would substantially reduce Euro-banks' gross lending spreads. Although such premia continue to be charged to individual banks, Euro-banks as a whole have resisted paying significantly over the offered rate for funds. In addition, pricing flexibility to preserve gross margins has been created either by a Euro-bank insisting on using its own LIBOR when it lends directly to a customer or by using a blend of individual LIBOR rates, including those of smaller institutions, to price larger syndicated credits. A related issue with which the Euro-banks have successfully dealt is that of the recycling of OPEC money in 1974–5. While only a limited amount of OPEC funds has flowed directly to Euro-banks, the large US and European institutions which are the principal direct recipients of such funds have in turn recycled these funds — after taking the appropriate turn — to Euro-banks and other institutions.

8 The Outlook for Euro-Banks

An assessment of the future development for Euro-banks must take into consideration both the variables which are largely beyond the control of the bank's management and those factors which lie within their power to influence. The exogenous variables which will play a significant role in the Euro-banks' future are the state of the Euromarkets themselves and the attitudes of Euro-bank stockholders.

As by-products of the development of the Euromarkets, Euro-banks are dependent in large part on the market's size, rate of growth or decline, structure and current psychological state. Prognostications on the future of the international financial markets centered in London abound, and often, depending on the current state of sentiment, observers swing from a positive view of the Euromarket based on its growth, potential economic contribution, and institutional necessity to a negative one characterised by physical decline, transmission of inflation and other unpleasant national economic phenomena, and propagation of unsound credit practices. Over their relatively short period of existence, the Euromarkets have continued to produce great adaptability to changing circumstances, new lending techniques and practices, and an almost unchecked record of rapid growth — all of which seems to indicate that they have become a useful institution in a highly internationalised world economy. The events of the past few years, in particular the successful recycling of OPEC surpluses, have shown how unlikely is a 'drying up' or reflow of funds to national markets. It would appear that the market actually thrives on presumably adverse developments, and dire predictions as to the future of the market are continually proven wrong.

The Euromarket's success is a function of the strength and sophistication of the London money market mechanism, the ability to offer highly competitive interest rates in a variety of currencies, geographic spread with sub-markets throughout the world, the willingness to undertake new risks and establish new credit mechanisms, and a physical capacity which rivals that of most domestic financial markets. Its vulnerability lies in its dependence on the growth of international trade and investment, on the existence of a certain level of confidence and, to a lesser extent, the ability of national markets to offer a competitive service to borrowers. International trade and investment should continue to expand over the long term, albeit at a slower pace than during the decade to 1973, while the almost inevitable presence of institutional and administrative barriers to the free flow of funds among national markets should ensure that the Euromarkets retain their distinctive attractions of size, sophistication, responsiveness, relative cheapness and risk preference. One cannot exclude the possibility of a 1930s-type depression and collapse of the international financial system, although the Euromarkets' survival in 1974 would appear to confirm their ability to withstand stresses approaching the 1930s collapse in intensity.

The greatest threat to the market in practice has been the crisis of confidence of 1974 which resulted in a temporary significant shrinking of the interbank segment and a sharply modified risk/reward preference in the direct lending portion of the market. A similar or perhaps more serious blow to confidence in the future cannot be excluded, particularly if loss experience in the types of credits which have been popular in the Euromarkets is regarded as unacceptably high. The Euro-banks would naturally be among the first to suffer from the resulting likely retrenchment of the interbank market as well as the possible direct loan losses which precipitated the decline in confidence. Given the likely support in various forms of parent banks and central banking authorities, however, the impact of such a retrenchment would probably take the form of shrunken balance sheet footings and profits and consolidation within the structure of parent banks rather than actual failures.

Within this framework of continued development punctuated by possible declines stemming from a blow to confidence, the risk/reward ratio on Eurocurrency loans, which are the backbone of the Euro-banks' business, should fluctuate in concert with the level of optimism and appetite for new business of the 300 or so banks which participate in the market. The experience of the past decade following sharp declines in confidence and interest in new business in mid-1970 (Penn Central) and mid-1974 (Franklin and Herstatt) seems to indicate a gradual cyclical return of a borrower's market over several years after the initial cutback in lending interest, with a consequent lengthening of maturities and shrinking of interest spreads and front end fees. Bankers' psychological attitudes and willingness to extend new credits have had a major effect on loan terms in a market of several hundred banks where a limited number of major institutions can determine market terms by their willingness to obtain what they consider a desirable piece of business. In short, timing will play a key role in establishing the risk/reward composition of a Euro-bank's portfolio, and there would seem to be a long-term tendency for competition over time to create lending conditions associated with a borrower's market with the result that Euro-banks must assume a highly competitive market on balance over an extended period of time. The doubling of spreads and halving of maturities which occured in many cases in late 1974 gives an indication of the role which competition and confidence play in establishing Euro-lending terms and the possibilities open to Euro-banks of maximising profits through the timing of the growth of their loan portfolio.

The second major outside variable affecting the outlook for individual Euro-banks is the strategic priorities of stockholder institutions. The rapid development of the Euromarkets has been accompanied by a significant evolution of individual parent banks' strategic priorities and objectives. One such change could relate purely to the parent bank's domestic environment, such as a merger, substantial domestic loan losses, capital adequacy problems and a changed perception of the priority of international vis-a-vis domestic banking which could stem from these factors. A US regional bank which took up a minority stake in a Euro-bank in the late 1960s may well feel that in 1975, with rising US loan losses and pressure from the Federal Reserve to reduce overall commitments, it cannot afford to provide adequate support to its growing Euro-bank affiliate which would have to take place at the expense of its traditional domestic business.

Secondly, a parent's international priorities may well have changed over time. A European bank which took a 10 per cent share in a consortium in 1970 as its first overseas banking venture may well in 1975 have an international loan portfolio and level of banking skills which exceed those of its affiliate. A large US money centre bank which set up a wholly-owned merchant bank in London in 1972–3 to develop an asset mix of a non-commercial banking character in the context of rising stock market, real estate and other values might well feel in 1975 that, given the overall international outlook coupled with possible domestic problems, such an activity should be significantly reduced or modified.

International relationships also evolve; a stockholder grouping which made sense in the conditions of the mid-1960s could a decade later have become subordinate to, or actually conflict with, a more recent association or the parent bank's desire to establish its own identity. Finally, the actual results achieved by the Euro-bank inevitably colour the parent's attitudes. It would appear that return on invested funds, market reputation, and contribution to a programme of diversification or customer service are among the principal criteria used by parent institutions to evaluate their Euro-bank affiliates. A consistently below-target return on equity or the inability to offer successfully the desired services would thus naturally raise some questions in the parent's thinking about continued support.

Stockholder attitudes have been particularly sensitised in some cases by the gradual presumption in recent years of total balance sheet support by the market and regulatory authorities such as the Bank of England. While most stockholders of wholly-owned subsidiaries and consortium banks assumed from the outset that their reputation as responsible financial institutions required a level of support of their affiliates which went beyond that normally associated with a limited liability company, the 1974 confidence crisis and subsequent requirement by the Bank of

England for letters of support rendered this assumption quite explicit for all Euro-banks operating in the London market.

For a relatively small stockholder with its own domestic problems, this clarification in some cases may well have substantially modified the stockholder's attitude to the amount and type of business being carried on by the Eurobank affiliate.

The importance of stockholder support was brought out by the interviews analysed earlier in this book. The most immediate source of support, of course, is funding assistance. With adequate back-up facilities in the form of direct funding or the ability to sell loans to parent banks, management can not only sleep better at night but also run its dealing position more profitably in view of the lessened need to provide a full liquidity backstop. Secondly, the difficulty any new bank has in attracting deposits and quality loan business places a premium on relationships which can be provided directly or indirectly by parent institutions. Finally, in the highly competitive investment banking business, the origination and placing capability of a parent institution willing and able to pass this business and resources on to its Euro-bank affiliate can mean the difference between a successful or loss-making investment banking activity.

It would appear from the above that stockholders' attitudes and capabilities will be a major determining factor in the outlook for individual Euro-banks. Events of the past few years have seen a number of changes in stockholder composition of individual consortium banks as well as the outright sale of one such London-based bank to a single US bank buyer. Stockholder influence on activity in 1974—5 took the form in a number of cases of requests to halt or significantly reduce new business activity in addition to the understandable admonitions to improve loan quality and loan risk/reward ratios.

Changes in stockholder objectives and priorities have often proven difficult, however, to translate into major modifications of Euro-bank ownership, structure, capital size and type of business if more than one stockholder is involved. Each stockholder invariably has its own views on the importance of profitability, the quality of management, business strategy and priorities, with the result that decisions involving the buy-out of other stockholders, changes in management, increases in capital or significant changes in business strategy have often been deferred indefinitely due to the inability to reach unanimous agreement. Subjective views of a parent bank's image and prestige have forestalled decisions to close down or substantially reduce the activities of some consortium banks, and one has the impression that a consortium bank may only be closed down in the event of such a major event as the incurring of losses exceeding the capital base or failure or disappearance of the parent banks.

As mentioned earlier, business contributions in the form of introductions to corporate lending and deposit customers as well as placing power for affiliates engaged in the Eurobond business have enabled several Euro-bank subsidiaries and affiliates of US and Continental European banks to show returns on assets and capital funds well in excess of the Euro-bank average. Looking to the future, therefore, Euro-banks with parents willing and able to provide substantial funding, new business, deposit clientele and placing power are extremely well placed to succeed in the highly competitive Euromarkets.

In addition to these exogenous variables which help determine the outlook of the Euro-bank, there are those factors which can be influenced to a greater or lesser extent by management itself.

It is, of course, stating the obvious to point out that quality of management is a vital factor in the success of a bank. Management quality is particularly relevant, however, in a highly competitive market with hundreds of banks seeking the same qualified personnel, cheap and reliable deposit base, low risk — high quality loans and loyal placing power.

As in most financial institutions, a variety of general management qualities are important to a Euro-bank's success: ability to recruit, organise and motivate staff, develop good accounting and management information systems, control expenses, establish and implement a strategic plan, maintain good relationships with other banks and so forth. But there would seem in today's Euromarkets to be four critical variables within management's control which will have a major bearing on a Euro-bank's likely performance. On this performance will turn such vital questions as a Euro-bank's reputation in the market, with its resulting impact on factors such as the ability to attract interbank deposits and to syndicate loans, the view of regulatory authorities, and its acceptance and support by stockholders, who are vitally concerned with such questions as market image, profitability and ability to provide specialist services.

The first of these variables is the ability to generate quality business for the Euro-bank's own loan portfolio and for syndication to others. While acceptable risks and adequate returns can be achieved by a passive policy of only taking loan participation from other banks, over an extended period of time the incremental return from front end origination fees coupled with the enhanced market reputation associated with a bank known for originating and managing quality business may well mean the difference between a successful and an average Euro-bank. Total or primary reliance on loans syndicated by other banks often implies a less intimate knowledge of the customer, lack of access to the most attractive business which is likely to be retained by the originating bank, and often a lower return on loan exposure. A useful deposit relationship also often accompanies own-originated business.

In the extremely competitive Euromarkets, the more highly regarded public and private borrowers are heavily solicited by literally hundreds of international banks, many of which offer services and capabilities beyond the reach of Euro-banks. Long standing personal and corporate relationships in this context play a key role, and the more successful Euro-banks are either able to benefit from a long standing relationship between a customer and a stockholder bank or from a personal connection between one of its own management personnel and the client.

A second variable is management's ability to evaluate credits and minimise loan losses. While a truism for banks in general, it is particularly vital for Euro-banks which do not have the benefit of a cushion of many years of retained earnings, operate on relatively thin gross interest margins, and depend to such an extent on the goodwill of other banks for deposits at a market cost. Not only can a single loan loss wipe out one or more years of a Euro-bank's earnings, but the psychological impact of such a loss, particularly during a period of market nervousness, may well seriously impair the bank's ability to obtain interbank funds. Loan losses experienced in 1974 by several wholly-owned subsidiaries of American banks resulted in the change of senior management and complete restructuring of the bank's mission, usually away from a major direct lending role towards an investment banking concept. In this vital function of credit evaluation, the Euro-bank executive is confronted more than most bankers by the classic conflict of credit judgement and the need to generate new business.

A third critical variable is the reputation and capability of a Euro-bank's dealing team in the funding of the bank's assets and either avoiding dealing losses or hopefully making a useful mismatch or foreign exchange profit. The London dealing community is an intensely personal one, and individual dealer's market reputations are often instrumental in a Euro-bank's ability to obtain funds at an acceptable rate. Interest and exchange rate fluctuations of the 1970s have placed a premium on dealing skills, and the market constraints imposed on many Euro-banks during periods of nervousness as in 1974 often require an extra bit of market feel, technical competence and personal relationships to earn a given dealing profit than would be the case for a larger, more established institution.

Finally, the ability to earn significant fee and other non-interest related income is another variable which, as in the case of new business generation in the lending sector, will in many cases make the difference between an acceptable and an outstanding Euro-bank performance. While many Euro-banks have only recently begun to emphasise this type of income, the relative difficulty of attracting investment banking clients and the unique skills often required in successfully offering corporate financial and other fee-earning services would seem to indicate that only a fairly limited number of Euro-banks will be more than moderately successful in this business. The successful ones are likely to be those who will either inherit business and perhaps human skills from parent institutions or hire the limited number of qualified investment bankers prepared to leave a prestigious domestic investment bank in favour of a Euro-bank.

An analysis of these variables in the light of experience to date and chief executive interviews in the summer of 1975 point to a number of likely general trends for Euro-banks over the next few years. First, within a framework of overall expansion of the Eurocurrency market, Euro-banks as a whole should continue their growth and remain a significant factor in the international markets. The year-to-year development of the Eurocurrency market itself, however, will be slower than in its salad days of the late 1960s and early 1970s, primarily because of the likely slower future growth of world trade and investment. Perhaps more important, this more mature market will be subject to periodic lapses of confidence stemming from anticipated or actual losses or other problems, and Euro-banks will suffer more from the resulting market shrinkage than larger, better established national banks. As in previous periods of rapid international banking expansion which produced a new generation of international banks, such as the mid-nineteenth century and the period following World War I, there will be a definite fallout of some members of the Eurobanking community due to such factors as substantial losses incurred and changes in parent bank circumstances or attitudes. On the other hand, new Euro-banks will be established in the coming years. For the most part, their objectives will probably be more specific than has been the case in the past decade and will focus on geographic and functional sectors of activity which are perceived to have special interest for the stockholders.

Secondly, within this overall context, certain profitability trends will become clearer. As a general proposition, Euro-banks will produce a lower return on earning assets than major banks in national markets, including most of their stockholders. Returns on invested capital are also likely to fall below those of stockholder institutions, although the probable continuation of significant gearing disparities makes comparisons quite difficult.

As discussed earlier, this lower average return will largely be a result of loan losses which may well exceed domestic experience, lower gross interest margins stemming from the relative absence of cheap deposits and strenuous competition for quality lending business, and the difficulty for most banks of generating significant fee or investment banking income. By the same token, those banks which exceed the average level of profitability are likely to enjoy one or more of the following: low or non-existent loan losses; significant customer deposits for which market interest rates are not paid; and fee income from new loan and bond origination business, corporate finance and other advisory activities.

In an effort to maximise profitability, Euro-bank management can be expected to take a number of internal policy measures. First, many banks will reduce the portion of assets placed with other banks to increase the overall return on assets. While lip service may be paid to the need to operate on both sides of the market, profit pressures will oblige many banks to relay on parent institutions for liquidity and increase average asset yields. Secondly, attempts to cut operating costs may result in such measures as hiring freezes, the reduction or closing of unprofitable departments and efforts to reduce rental expense. Finally, an increasing number of Euro-banks will take a more rigid line on the question of minimum acceptable return on individual loan proposals, which may well result in their being relatively inactive during future 'borrowers' markets'. Efforts will continue to be made to maximise balance sheet leverage but in most cases the more mature Euro-banks have probably already reached what the Bank of England and stockholders consider a reasonable maximum.

On present form, the relatively profitable banks are likely to include the subsidiaries of large US banks, which represent the loan syndication arms of their parents, and affiliates of Scandinavian and Continental full service banks who provide a significant amount of commercial and investment banking business and placing power to their Euro-bank affiliates. Banks specialising in generating loans from active borrowing sectors such as Latin America, Eastern Europe and the energy industry should also enjoy relatively high returns during the period when these sectors are particularly active. Banks prepared to take equity stakes or equity kickers on project loans should benefit from overall favourable economic conditions or the profitability of the industries in which they have taken a special interest. In many such cases, Euro-banks benefitting from these advantages should provide returns on assets fully competitive with those of equivalent national banks.

A third trend for Euro-banks will be the rationalisation of types of activity. In recent years, most Euro-banks have opened up with the advertised intention of providing a full range of commercial and investment banking activities. The growing international operations of many parent institutions and the actual performance of their Euro-bank affiliates will probably lead to a narrowing of this product range in many instances. Greater concern will be focused on an individual bank's identity to differentiate it from parent and competitor institutions as well as providing a competitive business strategy. On the other hand, a number of the larger, older Euro-banks set up as medium-term lending institutions have already established their own momentum and identity in this sector and will continue to specialise in medium-term loans. Other institutions organised to channel funds to and from specific geographic or functional areas will retain this role as long as this flow of funds continues; if the need declines significantly, however, a change in strategy may be dictated. Finally, those Euro-banks established essentially as branches of full service parents to participate in a broad range of Euromarket activities will probably continue to offer a wide gamut of services.

In the case of many wholly-owned and consortium Euro-banks, however, lending activities will be regarded by parent institutions as duplicating or competing with those of the parents. In such cases, these banks may increasingly focus on fee earning or investment/merchant banking activities which represent a useful diversification move for the stockholders. Profitability may well play a significant role in determining product line. On the one hand, management and stockholders may regard Eurocurrency lending as a marginally profitable business and prefer to focus on other activities. On the other hand, the difficulties of personnel recruitment, developing placing power, and acquisition of quality corporate finance business may lead other banks to close down their Eurobond or corporate finance departments as an economy measure to focus on banking business. Such decisions will depend on the ability of stockholders to provide assistance, the Euro-bank's track record, and management's own strengths and weaknesses.

In each of the trends can be seen the critical importance of the attitude of stockholders. In the case of consortium banks with a large number of stockholders, dissatisfaction by individual stockholders with the rate of return achieved and the services offered by the Euro-bank may not be translated into action because of the inability to reach unanimous agreement with other stockholders. Even if major problems of funding or loan quality are encountered by a consortium bank, the consensus decision can be expected to be support and restructuring rather than liquidation. In one case of publicly acknowleged funding problems of a Euro-bank in 1974, that of Western American Bank, a major consortium bank, stockholders were prepared to buy a major portion of the bank's loan portfolio. In other cases, Euro-bank management by its personality and performance record may create a momentum and identity which stockholders prefer to retain as the most practicable course of action. Probably the greatest structural change, therefore, will be observed in wholly-owned subsidiaries where profit record, change in parent circumstances or objectives and relative ability to develop a useful range of services for the parent bank will largely determine whether the subsidiary Euro-bank will follow the line of development initially envisaged.

These wholly-owned subsidiaries can be restructured more easily than consortium organisations, although as in the case of the latter the parent's sensitivity to its market image may well result in the maintenance of a higher and broader level of activity than would otherwise be the case.

As indicated earlier, stockholders appear to evaluate their Euro-bank affiliates not only in terms of profitability but also in those of market reputation, the providing of a specific range of services to supplement those of the stockholders, and an association with a desirable group of co-stockholders. Thus, an unprofitable investment banking division of a Euro-bank affiliate may well appear justified to an ownership group composed of commercial banks.

The competitive pressures on Euro-banks as a whole are strong ones. In addition to the structural disadvantage vis-a-vis established international banks discussed above, Euro-banks are rarely leaders in market pricing, and the theoretical possibility exists of the larger international institutions undertaking a loan pricing strategy designed to price the smaller and less well established Euro-banks out of business. While they would undoubtedly suffer from such a pricing tactic, the Euro-banks can be expected to defend themselves by concentration in specialist business less affected by such price cutting, diversifying into non-lending activities, or simply abstaining from new business for a period of time. Realistically, however, a deliberate price cutting move of this nature aimed at Euro-banks is highly unlikely because of the involvement of virtually all major international banks in Euro-banks of their own and the knowledge that they would be cutting their own loan profitability as much as impairing that of the Euro-banks.

The physical location of Euro-banks has traditionally been a subject of great speculation, as potentially attractive traditional financial centres such as New York or completely new markets such as Singapore appear to threaten London's post-war dominance of the Euromarkets. The analysis in this volume has focused on Euro-banks active primarily in the London market because of the latter's physical and structural importance as well as the collective and individual importance of the Euro-banks based in London. Such an analysis undoubtedly does not give a full perspective on the operation of Euro-banks worldwide, although the issues described are generic ones for the sector regardless of location. While London's market share may decline further in the coming years due to the undoubted advantages of other financial centres such as market proximity and lower taxes or operating expenses, under present conditions a bank which wishes to participate actively in the international lending and deposit market must give London at least serious consideration before setting up a new organisation.

Individual Euro-banks may well move part or all of their corporate structure and operations from London in the future because of tax and operating cost advantages. A major shift of the Euromarkets out of London, however, would seem to require not only a significant deterioration of present operating conditions in the London market but also an attractive alternative, which to date to a certain extent has taken the form of Luxembourg on the basis of lower tax and operating costs. Should such a mass movement occur, however, one can assume that the present London market with all its advantages of communication, regulatory climate and presence of hundreds of market makers will be re-established in a single new centre rather than be scattered throughout the world.

In the meantime, regional centres such as Singapore and Luxembourg will continue to thrive on the basis of their proximity to major regional markets, cost advantages and other factors. Each of these markets, however, will continue to look to London for the foreseeable future as the major loan syndication centre and source of ultimate funds availability.

As a concluding note on this glimpse into the future, it is appropriate to summarise some conclusions drawn from the experience of earlier international banks and market structures going back to the Renaissance period. From an admittedly limited exploration of the published literature on early international banking, one notes a number of recurring themes which have led to the downfall of individual banks established to do international business. As so many Eurobankers recognised during the troubles of 1974, simple survival is a precondition to achieving the lofty goals usually established for Euro-banks at their foundation, and survival for many Euro-banks was a very real issue during the events of the past few years.

Looking to the future survival potential of Euro-banks on the basis of the experiences described in Chapter 1, one immediately is aware of the vital impact of political and economic events such as war and recession on the ability of international banks to survive, much less achieve stated objectives. The global recession of 1974—5 has made today's bankers more aware of their vulnerability to such events, and in the future Euro-bankers would be wise to build into their decision-making process the likelihood of at least an occasional economic or political disaster beyond their control with its consequent impact on sovereign risk, commodity, project and other loans.

Secondly, the theme of overconcentration of risk runs throughout the history of international banking disasters. Whether it be a particular sovereign risk or industrial sector, countless international banks have come unstuck because of overenthusiasm for a particular type of business. Once again, the recent problems of some of the more popular borrowing sectors in 1972—3 should bring home to international bankers in the future the possible correlation between current popularity and future oversupply and other problems.

A final theme relates to the quality of international bank management itself. In the past, experienced and inexperienced bankers alike were thrown into novel overseas lending situations involving less developed countries and financial structures as well as totally different types of risk and credit evaluation. Compounding these structural difficulties was the natural enthusiasm of the management of a new institution to make its own mark. Conditions in today's international markets are not significantly different, and the Eurobanker of today would do well to remind himself that he is building for the very long term and that opportunities which may appear attractive in the short term may jeopardise his survival. A subsidiary theme in the management issue is the extent and quality of guidance from home office or parent institutions. International banking history is replete with the failures of overseas subsidiaries or branches left to carry on alone without some form of surveillance from stockholders' representatives.

Postscript

In March 1976, roughly six months since this book was written, it may be useful to make a few observations relating to market developments and the financial results of those banks in the sample which had published their 1975 results.

The Eurocurrency market itself has continued its steady growth; the Bank of International Settlements estimates that a 12 per cent growth in foreign currency assets of banks in its reporting countries took place in the first nine months of 1975. It would appear that the wave of new entrants into the Euro-bank sector has subsided, as only two new Euro-banks — both consortia with regional specialisation — have opened their doors in London in the past year. The same credit problems still preoccupy Euro-bankers — REITs, tankers and country risk — although sizeable losses for the Euro-banks as a whole seem to have been avoided to date.

Somewhat over one-third of the forty banks in the sample — predominantly the newer banks — had reported 1975 financial results by early March. Gearing levels for the newer banks understandably increased, while few changes over the 1975 levels were to be noted for the older banks. For the fifteen banks for whom figures were available at the time of writing, the deposits/capital ratio rose from an average of 11.0 in 1974 to 13.2 in 1975, while the loans/capital ratio increased from 5.4 to 7.1. Loans to deposit ratios moved in both directions, but the average of the reporting banks, heavily weighted by the newer banks, rose from 55 to 59 per cent between 1974 and 1975. The average liquidity ratio for the reporting banks remained unchanged at 31 per cent. For all but one bank, pre-tax profitability as a percentage of stockholder funds rose; for the newer banks — which in most cases had been set up in 1973 — the increases were generally quite sharp, while modest improvement was shown by banks in operation for three years or more. On average, the reporting bank average pre-tax return rose from 9.9 to 13.2 per cent in 1975. Even sharper increases were shown in after-tax returns expressed as a percentage of total assets. None of the fifteen reporting banks showed an operating loss, while the average net return of the reporting banks increased from .31 to .54 per cent reflecting primarily sharp rises in profitability of the two-year-old banks. Only two banks showed a lower net return than in 1974.

If this improvement is maintained by the remaining banks in the sample, one may be able to demonstrate much more favourable earnings comparisons with national banks than would be suggested by the 1973—4 results. It would appear that many banks significantly increased their loan loss reserves during the year as did banks throughout the world. Perhaps the most significant conclusion to be drawn from these results is that a period of perhaps five years or more must pass before a consistent earnings pattern for a new Euro-bank is established.

London
March 1976

Notes

Introduction and Overview

1 Paul Einzig, *Roll-over Credits — The System of Adaptable Interest Rates* (London, 1973) Geoffrey Bell, *The Euro-dollar Market and the International Financial System*, (London, 1973) Brian Scott Quinn, *The New Euro-markets* (London, 1975); and *Offshore Lending by U.S. Commercial Banks*, a publication of the Robert Morris Associates and the Bankers' Association for Foreign Trade (Philadelphia, 1975).

Chapter 1

1 Richard Ehrenberg, *Capital and Finance in the Age of the Renaissance* (London, 1928) p. 103.
2 Raymond de Roover, *The Rise and Decline of the Medici Bank* (Cambridge, Mass., 1963) p. 47.
3 Ibid., p. 95
4 Ibid., p. 121
5 Ibid., p. 264.
6 Ibid., p. 5.
7 Ibid., p. 372.
8 Ehrenberg, pp. 268, 270, 275.
9 Ibid., p. 93.
10 Ibid., pp. 103−4.
11 Ibid., p. 131.
12 Ralph Hidy, *The House of Baring in American Trade and Finance* (Cambridge, Mass., 1949).
13 Ibid., p. 146.
14 David Joslin, *A Century of Banking in Latin America* (London, 1963).
15 J. A. Henry, *The First Hundred Years of the Standard Bank* (London, 1963).
16 E. C. Corti, *The Reign of the House of Rothschild* (New York, 1928) p. 63.
17 Corti, pp. 110−12.
18 Ibid., p. 174.
19 Rondo Cameron, 'The Crédit Mobilier and the Economic Development of Europe', *Journal of Political Economy*, (Dec 1953).
20 Ibid., p. 470.
21 Ibid., p. 485.
22 L. H. Jenks, *Migration of British Capital to 1875* (London, 1927) p. 282.
23 Ibid., p. 49.
24 D. S. Landes, *Bankers and Pashas* (London, 1958) p. 52.
25 Victor Allen, 'The Prince of Poyais', *History Today* (Jan 1959).
26 Jenks, pp. 256−9.
27 Ibid., p. 291−2.
28 A. J. S. Baster, *The International Banks* (London, 1935) p. 61.
29 Ibid., p. 68.
30 Ibid., p. 165.
31 Ibid., p. 48
32 Ibid., p. 40.

33 Herbert Feis, *Europe, the World's Banker: 1870–1914* (New Haven, Conn., 1930) pp. 14, 16, 23.
34 Ibid., p. 210.
35 Clyde W. Phelps, *The Foreign Expansion of American Banks* (New York, 1927) p. 20.
36 Ibid., p. 131.
37 Ibid., p. 37; quotation from H. P. Willis, *Federal Reserve System* (New York, 1923) p. 1229.
38 Phelps, p. 164.
39 Siegfried Stern, *The United States in International Banking* (New York, 1951).
40 Ibid., p. 217.
41 Ibid., p. 224.
42 Hal B. Lary, *The United States in the World Economy*, US Department of Commerce (Washington, 1943).

Chapter 2

1 BIS, 45th *Annual Report* for period ending 31 Mar 1975, p. 131.
2 Morgan Guaranty Trust Co., *World Financial Markets* (New York, 1975), and private studies by David Ashby of Bankers Trust, Co. (see Ashby, 'The 300 Billion Super-Dollar Market', *Banker* (May 1974).
3 *Federal Reserve Bulletin* 'International Capital Transactions of the U.S.', (June 1975) Table 19a.
4 *Banker* (Nov 1974) p. 1337.
5 *Outlook for International Lending by Banks in 1975*, Special Report of US Treasury, 15 July 1975, p. 7.
6 Bank of England *Quarterly Bulletin* (Sep 1975).
7 Andrew Brimmer and Frederick Dahl, 'Growth of American International Banking', paper (Dec 1974) Table 2.
8 'Foreign Banks in London' *Banker* (Nov 1974) p. 1395.
9 'The Top 300 in World Banking', *Banker* (June 1975).
10 'Luxembourg', *Banker* (Feb 1975).
11 Monetary Authority of Singapore, *Quarterly Bulletin* (First Quarter 1975).
12 'Singapore' *Banker* (Sep 1974).
13 'Hong Kong', *Banker* (July 1974) p. 805.
14 George Blunden 'The Supervision of the U.K. Banking System', Bank of England *Quarterly Bulletin* (June 1975) p. 188.
15 'Foreign Banks in London', *Banker* (Nov 1974).

Chapter 3

1 Fred Ruckdeschel, 'Risks in Foreign and Domestic Lending Activities of U.S. Banks', International Finance Discussion Papers, no. 66 (July 1975).

Chapter 4

1 BIS, 45th *Annual Report*, p. 131.
2 Steven Davis, 'Running a Mismatched Book', *Euromoney* (June 1975) p. 14.
3 'The Capital and Liquidity Adequacy of Banks', Bank of England *Quarterly Bulletin* (Sep 1975) p. 240.
4 Ibid.

Chapter 5

1 World Bank Group, *Borrowing in International Capital Markets* (Washington, 1975) EC-181/752.
2 Morgan Guaranty Trust Co., *World Financial Markets*.

Chapter 6

1 Andrew F. Brimmer of the Federal Reserve Board, 'American International Banking — Trends and Prospects' (Apr 1973).
2 Davis, 'A Buyer's Market in Eurodollars', *Harvard Business Review* (May/June 1973).

Chapter 7

1 *Offshore Lending by U.S. Commercial Banks*, Chapter 2: Alexander Wolfe Jr, 'Country Risk'.
2 Richard Cummings, 'International Credits — Milestones or Millstones', *Journal of Commercial Bank Lending* (Jan 1975).
3 World Bank Group, *Multinational Debt Renegotiations since 1956* (Washington, May 1973).
4 *Offshore Lending by U.S. Commercial Banks*, Chapter 13, by Professor Charles Williams.
5 Bank of England *Quarterly Bulletin*, vol. 15, no. 3 (Sep 1975) Table 9.

Bibliography

Allan, Victor, 'The Prince of Poyais', *History Today* (Jan 1959)

Ashby, David, 'The $300 Billion Super Dollar Market', *Banker* (May 1974).

Bank of England, *Quarterly Bulletins*

Banker 'International Banking' (Aug 1974)
> 'Foreign Banks in London' (Nov 1974)
> 'Singapore' (Sep 1974)
> 'Hong Kong' (July 1974)
> 'Luxembourg' (Feb 1975)
> 'Top 300 in World Banking' (June 1975).

Baker, S. C. and Bradford, M. Gerald, *American Banks Abroad — Edge Act Companies and Multinational Banking* (London, 1974)

Bank for International Settlements *Annual Reports*.

Baster, A. J. S. *The International Banks* (London, 1935).

Bell, Geoffrey *The Euro-dollar Market and the International Financial System* (London, 1973).

Bennett, Edward W. *Germany and the Diplomacy of the 1931 Financial Crisis* (Cambridge, Mass., 1962).

Blunden, George 'The Supervision of the U.K. Banking System', Bank of England *Quarterly Bulletin* (June 1975).

Brimmer, Andrew F. 'American International Banking, Trends and Prospects', paper (Apr 1973).

Brimmer, Andrew F., and Dahl, Frederick R. 'Growth of American International Banking — Implications for Public Policy', paper (Dec 1974)

Cameron, Rondo 'The Crédit Mobilier and the Economic Development of Europe', *Journal of Political Economy* (Dec 1953)

Corti, Egon Caesar *The Reign of the House of Rothschild* (New York, 1928)

Cummings, Richard 'International Credits — Milestones or Millstones', *Journal of Commercial Bank Lending* (Jan 1975)

Davis, Steven I. 'Running a Mismatch Book', *Euromoney* (June 1975). 'A Buyer's Market in Eurodollars', *Harvard Business Review* (May/June 1973)

Department of the Treasury (US) *Outlook for International Lending by Banks in 1975*, Special Reports, Office of the Assistant Secretary for International Affairs (Washington, 15 July 1975)

de Roover, Raymond *The Rise and Decline of the Medici Bank 1397—1494* (Cambridge, Mass., 1963)

Einzig, Paul *Roll-over Credits — The System of Adaptable Interest Rates* (London, 1973)

Ehrenberg, Richard *Capital and Finance in the Age of the Renaissance* (London, 1928)

Farley, T. M. *The 'Edge Act' and United States International Banking and Finance* (New York, 1962)

Federal Reserve Board *Federal Reserve Bulletin*

Feis, Herbert *Europe, the World's Banker: 1870—1914* (New Haven, 1930)

Henry, J. A. *The First Hundred Years of the Standard Bank*, 1963, Oxford University Press, London

Hidy, Ralph W. *The House of Baring in American Trade and Finance* (Cambridge, Mass., 1949)

International Bank for Reconstruction and Development *Borrowing in International Capital Markets*, EC 181—752 (1972—5) (quarterly publication) *Multilateral Debt Renegotiations*, EC 170 (1956—68).

Jenks, Leland Hamilton *Migration of British Capital to 1875* (London, 1927)

Joslin, David *A Century of Banking in Latin America* (London, 1963)

Landes, David S. *Bankers and Pashas* (London, 1958)

Lary, Hal B. *The United States in the World Economy*, US Department of Commerce (Washington, 1943)

Macmillan Report (Committee on Finance and Industry, June 1931)

Mathis, F. John (ed.) *Offshore Lending by U.S. Commercial Banks*, (Philadelphia, 1975)

Mohammed, Azizali and Saccomanni, Fabrizio 'Short Term Banking and Eurocurrency Credits to Developing Countries', International Monetary Fund Staff Papers (Nov 1973)

Morgan Guaranty Trust Co. *World Financial Markets*

Phelps, Clyde *The Foreign Expansion of American Banks* (New York, 1927)

Quinn, Brian Scott *The New Euromarkets* (London, 1975)

Ruckdeschel, Fred B. 'Risks in Foreign and Domestic Lending Activities of U.S. Banks', International Finance Discussion Papers, no. 66 (July 1975)

Singapore, Monetary Authority of *Quarterly Bulletin*

Stern, Siegfried *The United States in International Banking* (New York, 1951)

Terrell, Henry S. 'Some Current Topics in International Banking', paper presented to American Management Association (Apr 1975)

Valentine, Robert 'A Profit-oriented Approach to Liquidity Management', *Euromoney* (July 1973)

Virkunen, Matti 'Experiences of Consortia and other Cooperation Vehicles', Banking in an Integrated World — Lectures at the 27th International Banking Summer School (Helsinki, 1974)

von Clemm, Michael 'The Rise of Consortium Banking', *Harvard Business Review* (May/June 1971)

Woodland, D. L. *Foreign Subsidiaries of American Commercial Banks* (Houston, 1963)

Index